And Who Are You?

And Who Are You?

By Margaret Lashmar

First Published 2015

Copyright © 2015 by Margaret Lashmar

All rights reserved. This book or any portion thereof may not be reproduced or used in any manner whatsoever without the express written permission of the publisher except for the use of brief quotations in a book review or scholarly journal.

First Printing: 2015

Stonepoint Press

stonepointpress.co.uk

ISBN 978-1-326-18592-3

For Laurence

Introduction

I am Margaret Sylvia Lashmar. I am 69 years old and live with my husband Greg, in Essex. He is my help and inspiration, along with other members of my family, who have spurred me into going ahead with this book.

I have a daughter Mel, a grandson Laurence, who is two years old (or was when this book was started) and adorable, he takes up a lot of our time, which we don't mind at all. I am retired and enjoy baking, gardening and writing my journals on my garden, recipes and travel which are another inspiration for the book, all the things I never had time for when I was working. I love most classic drama on tv and radio. I always read, mainly fiction. My favourite authors are Margaret Dickinson and Annie Murray, but there are many more. For me, they have to have a good story, with good characters.

My reason for writing this book is because I think it is a good, real-life story which I hope people will enjoy reading, with some laughter and some tears, and with no offence meant to anyone, I love them all.

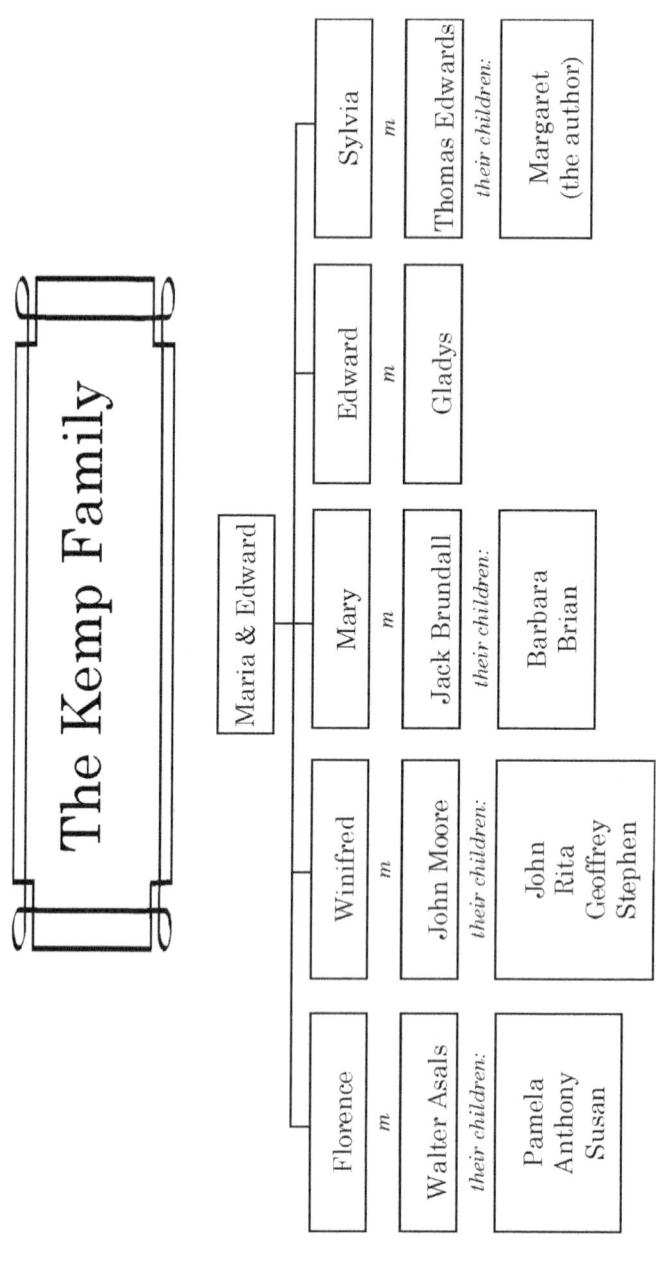

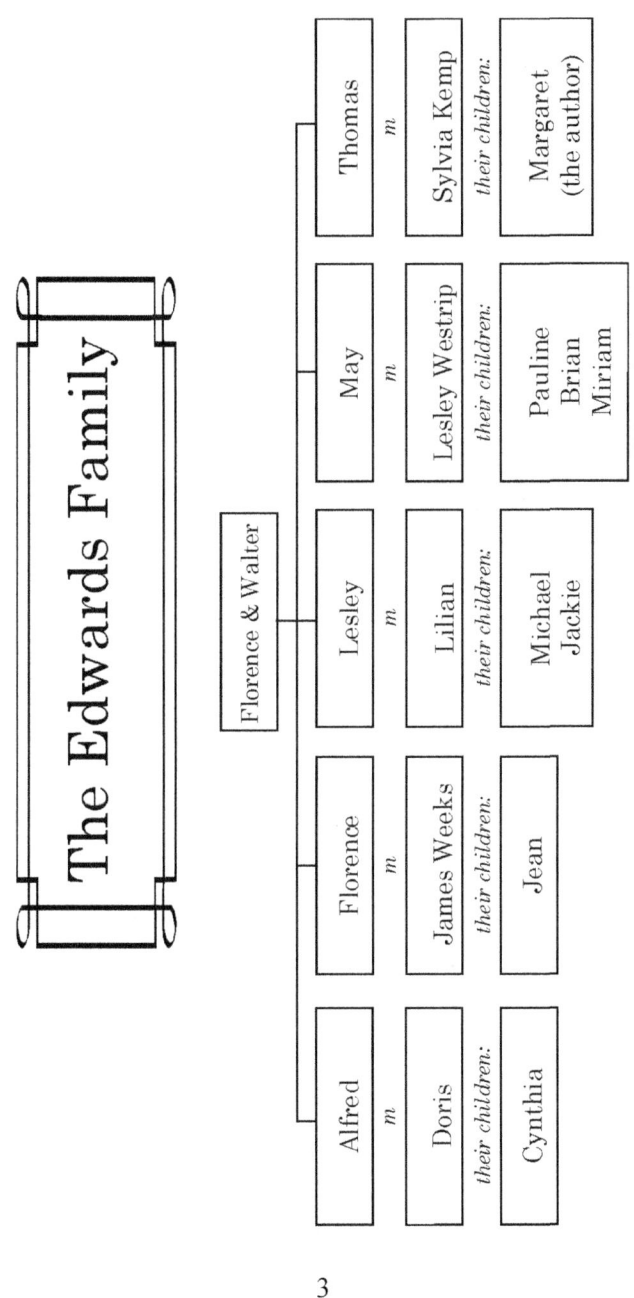

Chapter One

Thomas Henry Edwards, lived and worked in Enfield, Middlesex all his life. Enfield is just north of London. He was born on the 1st of January 1911, in Lincoln Road. They were terraced houses, usually two up, two down with an outside lavatory and a tin bath, which wasn't easy with five children in the household. It was lucky for him - he was the baby - he would go in the bath first, then it was the girls turn, Lord alone knows what the water was like after the boys had been in it. Actually he was quite lucky to be alive at all. His mother, Florence, fell down the stairs from top to bottom, while she was pregnant with him, with amazingly only bruises to show for it. He missed a lot of his schooling due to polio and was in a wheelchair for a long time, but he was such a determined little boy that he got to his feet in no time, but had to wear calipers on his legs. He wore the calipers until his early teens, but with the help of his family, his legs got stronger and stronger.

He was plagued with other illnesses, such as scarlet fever and rheumatic fever, which left him with a weak heart and brain damage. Doctors had to remove the damaged part of the brain and put a metal plate into the back of his head. He had a scar which went right around from one side of his head to the other, and he was in hospital for weeks. As a result, he again lost a lot of his education, but it never got him down. He always kept his sense of humour and had lots of fun with his two brothers, Alf (Alfred) and Lel (Lesley), his two sisters, May and Florence, (Flo - nicknamed Lol, by her husband, who affectionately called her 'lollypop', the family never asked why!) All the family spoilt Tom rotten, he was very handsome as a teenager, with a mop of dark, brown, wavy hair.

Thomas Henry Edwards

Tom went to work at Ediswans, a factory making domestic and commercial light bulbs, valves, small indicator lamps for telephone switchboards, large lamps for lighthouses and film studios. A very useful company during the war, the factory was situated at the end of Nags Head Road, (it closed down in 1967). Tom used to deliver parts of the lamps on his truck to the production lines, then when they were ready, he would then take them back to the stores for dispatch to the customers. He loved his job and would ride around on the truck singing away, always such a cheerful soul. At one o'clock he would cycle home to Aberdare

Road, Enfield. A spacious council house, with four bedrooms, a parlour, a big living room with a range fire and an oven (which they only cooked in at Christmas). Anyway, Tom would go home for his dinner, which would be something like meat pudding, veg out of the garden, and a heap of mashed potato, then apple pie and custard. His mum was a very good cook, how he ever managed to cycle back to work, they never knew, but he did, and his work mates were very envious when he told them what he had had for dinner. Because he was a handsome man he was never short of girlfriends, and it was mainly girls who worked at the factory.

After he had been working at Ediswans for some years, he had made enough money to buy a car. He bought a bullnose Morris, which he was very proud of. Although he couldn't drive, his brother, Lel could and they would take a couple of friends or his sister Lol and her boyfriend Jim out into the country. Places like Braintree, in Essex, where they would have picnics, and some light ale.

Tom, (front left), Auntie Lol (in cap),
her boyfriend, Jim (right), Uncle Lel (back right).

He would go camping with Lel and a friend, sometimes in a tent, but if they had enough money they would hire a caravan. Tom used to ask his mum and dad if they wanted to go to Southend, one of their favourite places, but his mum always said "no, thank you, it's an open top car," and that she "would get too cold," and they would go as usual, by train. Nan and Grandad used to go to places like Cliftonville or anywhere along the south coast where it was warmer. They would pack a small suit case each and go on the train to wherever they were going to stay, at a small seaside hotel. They were never ones for sitting in deckchairs on the beach. They liked to walk around or take bus trips, and sit on benches eating fish and chips out of the paper. In those days, the 1930's, it was white paper and real newspaper. If it was raining they would find a little café and sit down to a nice plate of steak and kidney pie, two veg and a pot of tea. That sounds like my kind of holiday even now. But when war broke out in 1939, the brothers were all called up for National Service. Tom was rejected because of his weak heart, although he was as strong as a horse. So the car had to go, and he went back to his bike, and kept driving his fork lift truck, which he was very good at.

Sylvia Dorothy Bessie Kemp was born on the 12th of March 1920 at St. Martins Road, Edmonton, North London. One of five, she being the baby. Her sister Flo (Florence), looked after her most of the time, as their mother was ill, sick with worry over the children and her husband who had been sent home from the Great War with shell-shock. He used to sleep with a bayonet under the pillow. Her mother slept with one eye open, because Sylvia slept in the cot beside him. She would say, "I don't think he would hurt her, but I keep one eye open just in case." He never really recovered, and would fly into rages, and take it out on her or the children. Flo was the angel, she could never do anything wrong. The family used to say "I wonder if she had the same father as us?" It was good that they had her there, to keep them all sane. There is a photo of them all standing outside the small, terraced house, in front of a notice on the wall saying '*Coke and firewood sold here.*' They all looked as if they had just been digging for it, like little ragamuffins, and I'm sure they had a hard life.

Edward (Ted), Win and Sylvia Kemp

As the years went on, all Sylvia's sisters and her brother left home and got married, and Sylvie was left at home. She went to work at Ediswans, as a clerk in the office, and at that time she was about 17 years old. She liked the work and made friends, one of the friends was Tom Edwards, the handsome fork lift truck driver, who would - in the stores, when the foreman wasn't watching - give her a ride on the truck. He would twirl it round and round, so she nearly fell off, it was such fun! They would go out to the pictures to see, usually a western film, with John Wayne, or Alan Ladd, or at the weekend a ride out in the Morris with Toms brother Lel and his girlfriend Lil. They would have picnics and beer, usually supplied by Toms mum, sandwiches, pies, and cake. They became quite close.

Just before war broke out, Sylvie's brother and brother-in-laws had been called up, so Mr and Mrs Kemp decided to evacuate their children, grand-children, and their friends children and grand-children to a rented cottage in Braintree, Essex. Sylvie didn't want to go, but because everyone else was going she had to. She was eighteen years old. So like the music hall song, they all packed into the van and off they went but without a 'cock linnet.' They stayed there for two years and although Tom visited her when he could, every time he went home she would cry her heart out, she so wanted to go home to Tom. After two years all living together, they had had enough, and as the bombing had eased off in London, they decided to go back to Enfield.

So... On the 17th of April 1941, Thomas Edwards married Sylvia Kemp at St. Michael's parish church in Edmonton. It was a lovely wedding and a beautiful dress. Sylv had three bridesmaids: her sister Mary and Toms sister Lol were the matrons of honour and Mary's daughter Barbara, who was about eight years old, and the apple of Sylvie's eye, was the youngest bridesmaid. There was a little page boy, John, also eight, who was Win's (Sylvie's sister) eldest son. Lel, Tom's brother was best man, which was only right, because he was his best friend too.

Photo on next page: Left to right: Auntie Lol, Grandad Edwards, Nanna Edwards, Uncle Lel, Tom, Sylvie, Nanna Kemp, Uncle Wal, Auntie Mary, Pageboy: Uncle John, Barbara.

They rented a house in Nags Head Road, a three bedroom terraced house with a 'best' room, which wasn't used very often, which was in the front; and a back room. Both rooms had open fires, down one step and into the kitchen, out through the back door there was an outside lavvy. The garden was one hundred feet long, and narrow, with some grass at the top end, and had a hedge all around it. At the end of the garden was a shed, then the back gate, leading to the alleyway, where the neighbours children used to play.

Sylv wasn't very happy living there. She wanted to live in Chester Gardens, which was the other end of Ponders End, in North London. A lovely road, and very quiet, where her sister Flo lived with husband Wally and daughter Pamela. Wally's family were middle class, so they could afford a better house. They were semi-detached, with an inside toilet and Sylvie longed to live in a house like that, but Tom was insistent that they couldn't afford to live there. "It's much too expensive in that area, if we bought a house in that road we wouldn't be able to afford any furniture." Her reply to him was "That's all right, we'll sit on orange boxes!" But Tom wouldn't have any of it.

While the war was on Tom was digging for victory. He dug up the garden at Nags Head Road and grew all the veg they needed, and he had an allotment as well. So he would go to work, come home, have his tea and then go straight to the allotment. Sylv, of course was bored with that, so she would get on her bike and go to her sister Mary who lived in Edmonton, it wasn't a long way, straight up the Hertford Road, turn into Church Street, then into Hyde Way. Mary lived at number one. Sylv would park her bike up against the wall, stroll in through the back door, calling out "Yoo hoo, its only me, Sylv. Just come for a cup of tea and a bit of bread and jam!" Mary would be sitting in the little living room, knitting up a jumper she had just taken apart, (bought from a jumble sale, wool was hard to come by during the war.) "Come in and sit yourself by the fire," - even in the summer, they would always have a fire, (most fires had a back boiler to heat the water) – and Mary would put the kettle on.

Auntie Mary Brundle (nee Kemp)

Jack, her husband, didn't go to war, he was a removal man, but he worked very hard. There was a lot to do clearing the houses after they had been bombed. He used to tell Mary of some horrible sights he encountered, so for relaxation and hobby, he grew raspberries and strawberries in the back garden, and huge chrysanthemums in the front, and he would make the most amazing jam. Holding a cup of tea in one hand and a slice of bread and jam in the other, Sylv would go on to tell Mary how hard she was finding it living with Tom "He never takes me out, not even to the pictures, or dancing. Before the war he loved to dance." Mary would carry on knitting. "With this war on, you don't want to be in those places (dance halls), you hear all the time about these places being bombed." Sylvie, would shoo the cat off of the big chair, and sit down, "Yes I suppose so. I used to go with Ted, up west, dancing, but now he has Gladys to dance with." Ted was Sylvies big brother, six years older than her, he later married Gladys and moved to Brighton. "I would quite like to have a baby, but Tom says not while the war's on. Lots of people have babies in the war with no problem." Mary stopped knitting and looked at Sylvie, "Be patient, your time will come." Sylv got up, looked at the clock, gulped her tea down, put the rest of the bread and jam in her mouth, and with her mouth full said, "I know, but I am so bored." They both laughed, "I had better be getting home, its getting dark, and Tom will worry, I'll see you soon." They kissed on the cheek. She rode her bike all the way home as fast as she could, out of breath, she called out. No answer. Tom was still at the allotment, she sighed, and got on to make the tea.

The war ended on the 8th May 1945, with great celebrations, and Tom and Sylvie had their chance to sing and dance to their hearts content. There was a great street party for which they made their costumes from old bridesmaid dresses, pageboy outfits, or make-do-and-mend 'posh clothes.' They had a great time and were so glad the war was over.

Remarkably all the men in the two families came home safely from the war; all but one, and that was Tom's brother-in-law Les, who had contracted tuberculosis, and just a few weeks after arriving home he died. He left Tom's sister May, and three young children; Brian, Pauline and Miriam, and with very little government compensation, they had to move out of their rented flat. The council found them a house in Brecon Road, just around the corner from Aberdare Road, where May's mother lived. Nice and handy for a chat and a cup of tea, all they had to do was find the rent. May did homework making necklaces of plastic popper beads, which didn't pay very much, so the elder children, Brian and Pauline, worked at them too. She had been living there about two years, when one day, just by chance, she met an ex-boyfriend, whose name was also Les, evidently a very fashionable name at the time! He was a widower and was looking for a room to rent, May said she had one, (the girls would have to share), Les moved in the next day, problem solved. Les stayed there for the next 20 years.

Chapter Two

Margaret Sylvia Edwards - that's me - was born at about six o'clock in the morning, on the 21st of October 1945, in the front room of Nags Head Road. It was a difficult birth and Dad said, "No more children for us, you are not going though that again." The family has told me that I was a grizzly child, quite shy, but quite pretty with dark brown hair and brown eyes, and that I looked liked my dad. Mum would dress me in pretty dresses, with ribbons in my hair and soft leather shoes and take me on the bus to Nanna Kemp's at St Martins Road, where we would meet up with her sisters for tea and cake. A lot of 'coo-cooing' went on. All of the sisters had young children by then.

Once I could walk I was taken everywhere on the back of mums bike. It saved on bus fares. Even then things were tight, money-wise. Mum talked to Dad about putting me into a day nursery and going back to work, he said he didn't want her to do that, so, she left it for a little while, then decided to give it a try.

The nursery was just across the road. I was only about two years old and mum took me over just to see what would happen. If I enjoyed it then she would go back to work. Well. What happened was, I screamed and screamed the entire time I was there, I got so upset, and Dad was so cross, Mum didn't dare do it again.

Dad was still at Ediswans and still growing veg both in the garden and at the allotment. The shed at the bottom of the garden was turned into a chicken house. Dad used to buy day-old chicks from Enfield Town Market, bring them home and put them in a seed tray in the fire hearth to keep them warm. I loved the chicks. Little, tiny, yellow, fluffy things and they would tweet away, driving mum mad. "Can't you put them chicks somewhere else?" she'd ask. "No," he'd say, "There's nowhere warm enough." I was glad, I enjoyed watching them all clambering over one another, they were so funny. I hated it when they had to be put out in the shed, to finish their growing. I was never allowed to watch when we were having chicken for Sunday dinner.

At three years old, I was always singing and dancing around the house. We had a long path from the back of the house to the back gate - which I was not allowed to go through without Mum or Dad. I had a two-wheeled scooter and would ride it up and down the path singing any old tune. That's when Mum decided to take me to dancing classes. I remember the teacher's name was Thelma. She was very nice and kind. My first routine was '*Me and My Teddy Bear.*' I picked it up so quickly that Thelma told Mum she wanted me to perform it in the show they were putting on in the canteen of the Rolling Mills in Brimsdown, Enfield. They made me a sequinned dress and hat, it was very sparkly, but not very comfortable, as it was itchy. I remember the pillbox hat kept falling off, so the lady who made it put elastic under the chin that was too tight - as you can see from the photo - I wasn't very happy wearing that costume. I was very happy performing on the stage and going to the dance school, I made friends with a girl called Gloria, and we used to do duets together.

My dancing debut. On stage in the staff canteen at Enfield Rolling Mills, with my friend Gloria

It was a big thing in the 1940's for factories to put shows on in their canteens. They were not very lavish productions, with country scenery painted on the backdrops, not many props needed, and just a piano for the music, but all the workers seemed to enjoy it while they were eating their food. It stopped them thinking about the war for an hour.

Another early performance, with yet more sequins!

During the late 1940's, things were still very hard-going. Rationing was still in force, so it was even more important that the family stuck together. We went to Nanna Kemp's every week and met up with my aunts and their children - my cousins - for the usual tea and cake - whatever they could get hold of, or make with what they had. Auntie Florrie seldom came, but Auntie Win, her son John and daughter Rita were there, and Auntie Mary with her daughter Barbara and son Brian, and Mum and myself. I was the youngest, Rita and Barbara were ten years older than me. Rita was very good at looking after me. Barbara was lovely, she had long dark, nearly black hair, very thick and shiny. She would ask Mum to brush it for her, "Go get the brush then." Babs would run and get the brush, sit in front of her and Mum would brush her hair for ages. It's a wonder she had any hair left by the time she'd finished. Me, I had very fine hair, two minutes and it was done. I was glad. I wouldn't have liked having all that brushing done!

The conversations over tea were about rationing; what meat they were going to eat for tea, and how long they were going to have to queue for it, and complaining about their husbands at which point Mum said "I wish Tom would find somewhere else for those damn chicks. They make a mess in the hearth, they smell and make a racket, but he says 'there's no where else to put them, they have to be kept warm.' Ha! He doesn't have to clean up after them." Mum never did like housework. Auntie Mary then piped up that she can't feed her chickens without her make-up on. "Why?" They all shouted. "It would put them off lay!" They all nearly choked on their tea with laughing. Auntie Mary never went anywhere without her make-up on.

Over tea one night dad said "I saw Jack today, he's just got out of the Merchant Navy and needs somewhere to stay. I told him we had a spare room he could use, if he wanted to and he said that would be grand." Dad knew Jack, but I don't know where from. I don't think they were friends as such, just acquaintances. Anyway, Mum said "Oh, do we have to take a lodger? The house is not your own with strangers in it." Dad said "Jack is not a stranger and anyway he will help with the bills." With a sigh, getting up to clear the plates Sylvie said "Right. I will clear the back bedroom. When is he moving in?" she asked. "Tomorrow," says Dad. "Oh hell! You might have given me some notice. I had better get started." She ran upstairs, leaving Dad and me laughing.

The next day after Dad had finished work he came home with this man, Jack. Rugged-looking with a long, bushy beard, a rucksack over his shoulder. "Hello Sylv how are yer? It's good of yer to put me up. I promise I won't be any trouble." Mum, eyeing him up and down replied "Come in Jack, I'll put the kettle on. I've a meat pie in the oven for our tea, why don't you go and unpack your bag while its cooking. It's the bedroom at the top of the stairs." "Righto, I'll do that. Well! Who's this then, looking at me?" "This is my daughter Margaret. Say hello to uncle Jack," she said looking at me. I never said anything, I wasn't sure I liked this man. The beard made him look a bit scary. "That's all right," said Jack "she's just shy," and went upstairs.

It was 1950, and I was five years old. I was going to Southbury Infants and Junior School. Mum would take me on the seat on the back of her bike. I was eating a slice of bread and jam, as we were usually late it was easier to eat on the way to school but by the time I got there I had jam all over my mouth. Mum would take her hanky out of her pocket, spit on it and wipe my mouth. Yuk! I hated that. I would rub the back of my hand across my mouth to rub away the spit. The school was a big, daunting, Victorian building. The tall, iron gates were hard to push open. We went in through the side doors, where the cloakroom was, and I was thrilled to have my own peg, which had my name on it: Margaret Edwards. It made me feel so grown-up. It was such a huge building. I used to skip and pretend to be a dancer, hold my skirt out and twirl around all the way down the long, wide corridor. I don't remember much about the teachers or the lessons, but I loved the school, and didn't mind being there until three o'clock in the afternoon when mum would pick me up on her bike and take me home, where we would have tea and more bread and jam. We seemed to live on bread and jam. I didn't mind, I loved it then – and still do.

I never looked forward to coming home. I hated Jack. He was always playing the fool, which Mum liked, but Dad and I didn't find funny at all. We thought some of it was downright cruel, like shaking the seed tray to frighten the chicks. Mum would laugh, dad would call him a idiot. Jack didn't like that, and would put his fists up to hit dad. Dad was strong. "Come on then" he'd say, and Jack would just laugh. He didn't want to be thrown out, he was too comfortable. I just cried. At the weekends dad started working in the back garden instead of going to the allotment. I didn't know why, but I was glad he did. I would help him as much as I could. When he dug the holes in the ground for the potatoes, I would pop them in the holes.

"Am I being a help Daddy?"

"Yes," he'd say, "A very big help Margarita." That was his pet name for me. I think he wanted to have me christened with that name, but Mum didn't like it, so they compromised and had me christened Margaret. Margarita was dads special name for me and it always made me smile.

One weekend when Dad was in the garden and I was riding up and down on my scooter singing, mum and Jack came out to see what we were doing. It was a nice day but it had been raining earlier and the hedges and trees were wet. I rode towards them, and when I got to Jack he whisked me up and plonked me in the hedge. I screamed, mum and Jack laughed. Dad was furious, dropped his spade and came and got me off the hedge. "You stupid bloody fool! Why don't you grow up?" He looked daggers at Jack. "Don't be such a grump Tom. It was only a joke. You spoil her too much." Mum took me indoors to dry me off. At bedtime Mum always said "Kiss uncle Jack goodnight." I wanted to shout 'no, I hate you!' But I didn't, I put my cheek to his beard and let him kiss me. Once in bed I would rub and rub at my cheek to rub him away.

One afternoon, when Mum picked me up from school, instead of going straight home she went to Nanna Kemp's. It was the day that all the sisters were there, and I didn't know at the time that she had something important to tell them. When they were all sat down with their tea she said "I'm leaving Tom and going away with Jack." Everyone sat there, stunned. "You're not serious?" "Yes Mary I am. I can't stay with him any longer. I don't love him any more, I love Jack, and he makes me laugh. The only thing is he wants me to leave Margaret with Tom. He won't take her with us. He is an engineer, and we will be travelling around a lot, and that's not suitable for a little girl. I am here to ask you to help Tom look after Margaret. Will you do that for me please? I can't stay." Win said "Are you sure you know what you're doing? Tom's a good man and he loves you." "I'm not sure. I know Tom loves me and I don't want to leave Margaret behind, but I have to go." Nanna said "When will you go?" Mum said "As soon as we can." Nanna put her arms around Mum who by now was in tears. "You take care of yourself, if you need us we will be here for you." They all hugged, said goodbye and waved us off. She did manage to speak later to Auntie Florrie who tried to stop her from going but it wouldn't make any difference. I knew nothing of this at the time, and this story was related to me much later.

The day Mum left was for me just an ordinary day, Mum took me to school as usual, I was there all day until three o'clock, and Mum was waiting for me outside the gates.

"Have you had a nice day darling?"

"Yes," I said.

She strapped me into the seat on her bike and off we went home, when we got home she said "You take your bread and jam into the living room I have to do something upstairs." I sat down on the floor in front of the fire, and after a little while, I heard Mum come down the stairs, into the hall, open the front door and close it quietly behind her, I jumped up and went to the door I could just about reach to open it, I ran out, I could see her walking down the road I shouted after her

"Mum where are you going? Can't I come with you?"

"No darling," looking round at me, "You have to stay with Daddy, he will be home soon. Go and play with your toys."

I stood there watching as she disappeared round the corner. I thought maybe she was going to get something for our tea, so I went back indoors, shut the door and waited for dad to come home. I didn't have to wait long. When I heard the key in the door, I ran out to him.

"Hello, Margarita. Where's your Mother?" he said.

"She's gone shopping, she had a case with her. She said to wait for you."

"OK, you go out and play on your scooter, I'll be there in a minute."

I went running into the garden relieved to know that dad was home. It seemed like hours that I had been in the garden, I was hungry and it was getting dark, so I went indoors. It was dark inside, and I walked through all the rooms, feeling a bit frightened, hoping Dad hadn't gone too. What would I do? Who would get my tea? I would have to go to Mrs Branch's, next door. But when I got to the front room, there was dad in the dark, crying, with a note in his hand, I didn't say anything, and he just looked at me.

"Mum has gone away with your uncle Jack, she won't be coming back."

I thought, I'm glad Jack's gone but I wish mum hadn't gone too. We both went into the living room and sat by the fire, no one spoke.

I never knew what was in the note, dad threw it on the fire. He sat in the chair, staring at the fire, I sat on the floor playing with my toys and the chicks. I was hungry.

"Are you hungry?" I said to dad.

"No," he said "But you must be. Would you like some milk and biscuits?"

"Yes please."

He got up from the chair slowly, put the kettle on to make some tea for himself, then fetched me a glass of milk and two biscuits. The milk was too cold and the biscuits were arrowroot, not one of my favourites, but today they were lovely. Dad sat down with his tea, and I curled up by the fire, dad put a cushion under my head. If mum was here I would have been in bed by now, but I don't think dad wanted to be on his own. We didn't speak, and I was nearly asleep when suddenly there was a knock on the front door.

"Who can that be? You stay there I'll be back in a minute"

I sat up waiting to see who it was. What a shock to see mum coming in.

"Mummy!" I shouted, and she scooped me up and swung me round.

"I couldn't go and leave you." Dad made some more tea, and mum sat with me on her lap. "Why aren't you in bed, young lady?" she said.

"Dad needed my company," and we all laughed.

"When you've drunk your tea I'll go and get us all some fish and chips."

"Oh yes, please!" I piped up. That was my favourite tea – and still is. It was nice to have mum back, everything could go back to normal.

Dad was just about to put his coat on, when someone knocked on the front door again, dad went to the door.

"Where is she?" I knew that voice, it was Jack. Mum put me down on the floor and went to the front door.

"I'm not coming with you Jack."

"That's what you think. Out of my way Tom, I don't want to hurt you." He pushed Dad out of the way, but dad stopped him getting past.

"You heard what she said."

I was told later that Jack pulled a knife - how true this is, know one knows - I was just getting up, when I caught my foot on the fender, fell forward and hit my head on the fire grate, and then I screamed. Luckily the fire was nearly out, otherwise I would have been burnt. Dad came rushing in, picked me up and rushed out of the front door. Mum and Jack had gone. Mum looked back, saw that I was alright and went on, with Jack dragging her behind him.

My head was bleeding, not very much, but enough for dad to put a plaster on it. I still have a scar, just a small one. He carried me up to bed, I put my nightie on and got into bed, and he said "Goodnight Margarita" but I was asleep before I could say goodnight. It had been a long day. If the story about the knife is true, without knowing it, my scar might have saved dad's life.

When I woke up the next morning I jumped out of bed and ran downstairs to see if mum was there. She wasn't. Everything felt different, but tea was on the table, so was the bread and jam, I opened the back door and looked out to see Dad coming up the path.

"Hello Marg. I've been down to feed the chickens, go and get dressed, and have your breakfast. I've arranged for Mrs Branch to take you to school. I have to go to work, so be ready when she comes for you."

I did what Dad told me. I could see he was in no mood to argue. Mrs Branch was nice. She was our next-door-but-one neighbour, she would do anything for you. If dad was working in the garden and she was out there too, she would have a chat over the fence. She had once or twice taken me to school before, but she didn't have a bike, so we had to walk. It wasn't a long way, but for a little girl of five and a half, nearly six, it was. My legs were too tired to skip down the corridor of the school that day. Mrs Branch said she'd pick me up after school and take me back to her house until dad got home, and she would give me my tea. So this is what happened every day until the weekend came.

Grandad & Nanna Edwards

Then we would go to Nanna and Grandad Edwards house in Aberdare Road. I liked it there, but they didn't have any chickens. Dad had to go back every day to Nags Head Road to feed them, sometimes I would go with him and sometimes I would stay at Nanna's and help her mangle the washing. This is how we lived for the next few weeks. Sometimes I stayed over at Mrs

Branch's with her daughter Gillian. She was good to me, and we shared a bedroom. If she could see I was upset she would come and sit on the bed with me, "I'm sure your Mum will come back soon," she'd say, putting her arms around me. "I hope so," I'd reply, for although they were all very nice, I just wanted everything to be back to normal.

Everything changed again when I got sick with one of the children's diseases, I don't know which one. Anyway, Mrs Branch had to take me to the doctors. Just by chance Dads sister, Auntie Lol was there.

"Hello, Mrs Weeks," Mrs Branch said sitting down. "I'm glad I've seen you. Have you heard the news? Sylvie's left Tom, and gone off with that lodger and left Margaret behind. Now she's ill, and I have to go to work. I have had to take the day off today to bring her here. I was wondering if you could look after her until she's better?"

"Of course. Leave her with me," said Lol. "I knew this would happen. Tom was far too soft with that woman." Auntie Lol continued, taking my hand.

"Thank you," Mrs Branch stood up ready to go. "I'll tell Tom she's with you." She bent down and gave me a little kiss, "you'll be staying with your Auntie for a little while until you're better. All right?" I just nodded.

While I was recuperating at Auntie Lol's, arrangements were being made for Dad and I to move in with Nanna and Grandad Edwards at Aberdare Road.

Chapter Three

Aberdare Road was a very different house from Nags Head Road. It was a semi-detached, council house in, what was then a long, quiet road. All the houses were the same, well looked after by the council. You walked in the wrought iron gate into a small front garden with a hedge around it. You could go round the back, which we did most of the time, into the large back garden, which like Nags Head was put to vegetables because of the war, except for a small piece of grass with an apple tree in the middle, where I would play a lot of the time. Mummies and daddies, with dolls and teddies.

When you entered the back door you were in the scullery. Quite small, with a butler sink, a large copper for doing the washing and cooking the Christmas puddings, a mangle, and a recently installed 1950's style gas cooker, which Nanna was dubious about using first of all. Grandad liked it, at least he didn't have to light the range oven every day.

The range was lovely, we used to light the fire every day - it had a boiler at the back for heating the water - although they used to have the big kettle on the top of the range for making the tea or washing the dishes and pots and pans. They could have used the gas, we even had hot water coming out of the taps, but they didn't like change, so they stuck with what they knew. The kettle was so heavy, that me, at seven years old couldn't lift it.

It was a lovely cosy living room, with a big table in the middle, a walk-in larder, which most of the time was full of food. Nan was a good cook. It's funny really, the room was always warm, but the larder was always freezing cold.

Out of the living room past the front door and into another small room which was the 'parlour.' This room was used for high-days and holidays, big parties at Christmas. The only furniture in it was a few chairs, a piano, and of course an open fire.

Upstairs, there were three bedrooms. Nanna and Grandad had the big one, Dad had the next biggest, and I had the little one, which faced the back of the house, so was freezing. In fact the whole of the upstairs was freezing. The only good thing about the house was, we had an inside toilet and a bathroom. The downside of that was you had to carry the hot water from the scullery up to the bathroom if you wanted a bath. If we did, we always waited until Dad was there, because he was the only one strong enough to carry the buckets up the stairs! You had to carry about half a dozen enamel buckets full of hot, nearly boiling water to get about seven inches of water, which is all you were allowed, because rationing was still on. He would huff and puff every time. I was allowed to go in first, then they would toss a coin to see who would go in next, great fun. In the winter you wouldn't stay in too long anyway, it was too flipping cold.

It must have seemed strange for Nanna and Grandad when we descended on them. They were both getting on in years, in their late sixties, I think, but bless them, they didn't seem to mind. In fact I think it helped Nan. She was still taking in washing when we moved in, and she had rheumatoid arthritis. Her fingers were bent up, and quite painful I would imagine. There were no treatments, you just took aspirin for the pain. I think it was taking in the washing that was some of the cause. So now Dad was paying housekeeping money for us to live there, Nan could stop taking in washing.

Grandad was a nice man and he was a good cook. Rock cakes, and Christmas puddings (which were very boozy, but very good,) were his speciality. The one thing I remember about him was that he used to wear false teeth. National Health ones. He would only wear them when he went out or whenever we had visitors. Whenever he was called when a meal was ready, he would say "Just a minute, I have to take me teeth out." "Oh, hurry up!" Nan would say, "Your food is getting cold." He would never wear his teeth for eating, in fact if he could get away with not wearing them at all, he would. I always thought he looked better without them anyway.

Me, aged about four or five

I grew up very quickly, became independent. I walked to school, which was just around the corner. I never went to school without breakfast. Porridge, then egg, bacon and toast or fried bread, and a mug of tea nearly as big as me. I could only ever drink half of it. No wonder I never wanted my school dinner, they were horrible anyway. So Nan said "Would you like to come back for your dinner? Your dad does, so you might as well." "Yes please." I said, I knew Nanna's dinners were always good.

I was in the juniors now, we had to go into the other gate, which wasn't so impressive as the infants gate, and again into the side doors, same corridor. I looked down to the other end, the infants, where Mum would bring me in. I didn't feel like singing or skipping now. In fact, juniors was a bit of a blur all together really. I do remember being bullied. Not so much physical - a bit of hair pulling - but I just pulled theirs back, of course they would scream and I would get into trouble, but I could put up with that, after a while that stopped. No, the one I couldn't cope with was the mental bullying. When they would say that it was because of me that mum left, that I was a trouble to her and she couldn't cope with me. One of the culprits was a cousin of mine, Miriam, Auntie May's daughter. She got involved with a family who lived across the road from the school, troublemakers. Miriam was desperate for friends. We tried to be friends, but as soon as the others showed up, she was on their side, so I knew that she was no true friend.

I did have a good friend in the juniors and her name was Betty. She used to come and stay with me at Aberdare Road. We would play shops on the big table in the living room. Betty was a very forthright girl and one day asked Dad "Why did Margaret's mum leave her? Was it her fault?" "Of course not," said Dad, "Why do you ask?" Then Betty told him about what the girls had been saying and who they were. Dad said he would have a word with the headmaster. I was terrified to go to school for the next few weeks, wondering what would happen. I needn't have worried. The troublemaking family were moved out of their house and out of our school. Apparently, they had been making trouble somewhere else also. As for Miriam, she kept out of my way and I kept out of hers.

It was 1952. No one ever spoke of mum, but I knew there was something going on. Grandad was telling Dad that he had gone to St. Martins Road.

"I'm sure I saw her Tom, walking down the road, holding a little boys hand. You know she's not coming back don't you? You must get a divorce." He said.

"I don't want a divorce," said Dad, "She might come back, otherwise what would she be doing down this way? I'll speak to Mary, if Sylv were to get in touch then it would be her she'd contact. Anyway. I'm thinking of buying Nags Head Road."

"Whatever for?" Grandad said looking at Dad quizzically, "I would have thought you would want to get rid of that house."

"No Dad, if Sylv comes back we will need somewhere to live. In the meantime, I will rent it out. There's a couple I know who have just moved here from Scotland and are looking for a house to rent. They are willing to wait until the house sale has gone though, then they will move in."

"Well! I'll leave it to you then son." Grandad said shaking his head.

I sat there listening.

"Does that mean mum's coming home?" I said jumping up and down.

"No." They had forgotten I was there. "No. Sorry Margaret, not today." Dad said, I slumped back into the chair.

Every Sunday Dad and I would go to see a friend of Dad's. A lady friend. She lived in Chingford, Essex. I didn't know her name - we always called her 'Chingford Lady' – and she was very nice. We would get on the bus just across the road at the bus station. I was always fascinated by the bus conductor with his ticket machine. Dad would give him the money and he would wind the handle and out would came a ticket. Then if we were very lucky a ticket inspector would get on, and say *'Tickets please!'* We would show him our tickets, he would punch a hole in it and give it back. Very exciting, for a seven year old.

Chingford Lady always did a lovely tea, corned beef and tomato, and tinned salmon and cucumber sandwiches, and a nice, light fruit cake. Then Dad and her would go to the kitchen and talk, and I would sit and listen to the wireless. Sunday night at seven was *'Sing Something Simple'* with the *Cliff Adams Singers.* I learnt a lot of songs from that programme, and I would dance around the room holding my skirt out. When the programme finished we said goodbye and caught the bus back home, I would fall asleep and Dad would have to carry me home. I would have a glass of milk and take myself up to bed, I'd go to sleep with the songs from the radio in my head.

The Chingford trips got less and less until they stopped all together. The talk in the family was that there was talk of marriage, but Chingford Lady had said she was too old to take on a little girl, so that was that.

To replace our Sunday outings to Chingford, if the weather was good, Nanna and Grandad would take me on the train to Southend for the day. Nanna would buy me a big brimmed straw hat and I would skip along the sea front, singing. I would ride on a rocking horse, then we'd get fish and chips, find a bench and eat it out of the paper, what a treat!

Me on a rocking horse, Southend-on-Sea

Chapter Four

The summer of 1952 was our first real holiday. Dad had got two weeks off from the factory. Auntie Win and her family had moved to the Essex coast to run a boarding house. She said to Dad "You and Margaret are very welcome to come and stay as long as you don't mind where you sleep. Most of the rooms will be full." "That's all right." said Dad and made arrangements for the last week in July and the first week in August. He booked the coach, which we had to pick up from Chingford.

I was so excited, I couldn't sleep. I had never been on a coach before. We caught the bus to Chingford, then waited at the bus stop for the coach, five minutes and it was there. I had never seen anything so big and I had a job to get up the steps. The driver said "Come on little lass," and helped me into the the coach. He showed us into our seats. They were huge, and I sat there like a princess on a big throne. Then we were off. It seemed to take forever, then all of a sudden we stopped.

"Are we there, Daddy?" Feeling excited, but a bit queasy.

"No," he said, "This is only half-way. We've stopped for a drink and the toilet."

"Oh! How long does it take?"

"About three hours," Dad replied.

"*Three hours,*" I said looking disappointed, "I feel a bit sick."

"We'll get some barley sugar sweets, that will help. You run off to the toilet now, we will be off again soon."

While I was gone Dad asked the sweet lady if she had any sick bags for me, she laughed and said she had. On the second half of the journey, I needed both the sick bag and the barley sugars.

When we got to Walton-on-the-Naze, Auntie Win and Rita met us off the coach.

Rita said, "You look awful Margaret, are you all right?"

"I was sick and Dad gave me barley sugars, it was such a long journey, are we here now?"

"Yes," Rita said laughing, "Come on."

We walked to their house. It was good to walk after all that sitting down. There were a lot of people in the house I didn't remember; Uncle John, and Geoffrey and Stephen, their sons, Rita's brothers. Stephen was a year or two older than me, and they were all sitting around the kitchen table. There were lots of comings and goings – people and dogs - they had two; a bearded collie, and a small terrier, which was always jumping up and scratching me and making me cry.

Auntie Win said to Dad, "I've put a camp bed up in the garage for you Tom, I hope you don't mind, all the rooms are full."

"That's fine," he said. I don't know how he slept in there, it stank of petrol, but he was glad of the holiday. I expect he paid his way. I slept down the garden, in a big shed. It was sectioned off, one half was for Geoffrey and Stephen, and the other was for Rita and me. I had to get undressed in the kitchen and run down the garden to the shed. The only problem with that, was that Auntie Win kept geese. Rita would go down to the shed first, then say to me "Come on, but don't run because they will chase you." So I would start to walk quite calmly until I got about half way down then they would run after me and bite my nightdress. I would run as fast as I could into the shed, Rita said laughing, "I told you not to run." "But they were biting my nighty,' I said. "That's all right, they won't hurt you," Rita said. I'm sure she did it on purpose. This happened every night for two weeks!

While I was sleeping the grown-ups would be discussing what Dad should do about Mum. Auntie Win said "I think you should think about a divorce Tom, she has been gone quite a while now, hasn't she?" Uncle John said "I think they're in Ireland." "Why do you say that?" Auntie Win looked puzzled. "Well, he's Irish isn't he?" Uncle John looked at Dad. "I don't know, not that I'm aware of. Anyway, I don't want a divorce, but everyone I talk to says I should go ahead with one, so I have. The solicitor says that Jack will be due to pay £200 in damages and costs and £200 in back rent. At the moment they don't know where they are, the courts are putting an agent on to it." "There you are, what did I say? They've done a bunk to Ireland!" said Uncle John trying to lighten the proceedings. "I'm sorry Tom for you and that little girl, we will do anything we can to help." Uncle John got up from the chair, "I think a drop of whisky is called for." "Thank you for putting us up. I think Margaret has enjoyed the holiday," said Dad taking a big swig of whisky.

This story was told to me by the family when I was a bit older and could understand what was going on. I did enjoy the holiday. I enjoyed playing on the beach with my bucket and spade with shoes and socks on. I didn't like playing on the beach with bare feet or paddling in the cold water. My cousin Rita says I used to hold my legs up and would not put them down and scream until they took me off the beach.

It was hard to get used to the two families. Mums was very outward going. Busy working people trying to make a living. The house was always full of people and children and I found it hard to get used to. Whereas Dads family were much quieter and calmer. They still had fun but in a different way. I just had to get used to them. We spent many happy holidays on the Essex coast, but I never got used to coaches. We tried going by train. I liked it, but Dad didn't, we had to catch too many buses and trains. He preferred the coach, so I took my travel sickness pills and barley sugars. I always felt a bit queasy but was never sick again. I was always a thin, sickly, little girl.

On the beach, Walton-on-the-Naze. Note the shoes and socks!

On the 18th of September 1952, Mum and Dad were divorced. The court agent was unable to find them. The last information from him was that they were living in lodgings in

Cambridge, but were intending to go abroad. There was no one at the lodgings when the agent went there. Nothing more was done about it, and Dad had to pay weekly instalments to settle the costs, which in those days was a lot of money. But to be honest Dad would have rather had Mum back, and so would I. It came to pass in later years that Mum had actually written to her sister, my Auntie Mary, asking if her divorce had come through as she wanted to marry Jack – quoting something to do with tax - and she was going to have a baby, and at the moment they were living in separate bed sits. This we think was in Cowley, Oxford. Auntie Mary didn't have an address just a Post Office box number. Auntie Mary was sworn to secrecy, because they knew the courts where after them and Jack was never going to pay the fines. Mum didn't want him to go to prison. So, Auntie Mary kept that letter secret for a long time, until well into my adult years.

During the winter evenings we would sit in the living room at Aberdare Road, or around the kitchen table, in front of the range fire, eating herrings and making toast with a toasting fork by the heat of the fire. We'd be listening to the wireless; *'Paul Temple'*, was one of my favourites, Dad liked *'Dick Barton Special Agent.'* We all loved the comedies, *'Dads Army, Round the Horn, The Glums'* and a host of others. On Saturdays, at five o'clock it was the football results, and I used to get really excited.

"Please can I fill in the numbers, Daddy?"

"Only if you're very careful. That coupon is worth a lot of money," he would say, passing me the coupon with a smile on his face.

"I will, I promise." I would wait until the man started saying the numbers, then I would write them down very carefully. He was good, he always went nice and slow and once we were done, I would pass the coupon over to Dad for him to check to see if we had won. I would pester him...

"Have we won? Have we won?" I'd keep saying.

"Give me a chance!" He'd say, "It has to be done properly." His head was always down, concentrating on the coupon. Most of the time we didn't win anything, but on one or two occasions we did win. Anything between £50 and £100, nothing more than £100. When we did win, I got really excited, as it meant I got a new pair of shoes, or a new dress.

Every Christmas I would wake up to a toy at the end of my bed. Never a stocking. I never knew what that was. One Christmas it was a 'walky-talky' doll. I called her Dolly, original eh? Her legs were very stiff and I used to have to walk behind her to help her walk. She was very pretty, with very long hair which I used to comb and comb until eventually it all fell out, then she had to wear a hat all the time. When I picked her up and turned her over she would say, 'Mama,' I did love her.

The next Christmas at the end of my bed was a teddy bear, when I picked him up he made a grumpy noise, hence he was called Grumpy. I did get other toys for birthdays and Christmases, like a toy farm, a shop and a post office. Nanna was a customer, buying pretend stamps, and postal orders and such like. Then there was my real china tea set, which I had to be very careful with, but it was lovely. In the summer Dolly and Grumpy and I would sit under the apple tree and have a tea party, Nanna would make sandwiches, and we would have real tea made in the teapot, we would have to wait until it cooled down before we poured it out in case I burnt myself.

Sixty years on, and the only toy I have left is Grumpy. He is in good condition, all but his nose, which was bitten off by one of our naughty puppies, he does still make his grumpy noise though.

In March 1953, Dad bought the Nags Head Road house,

and was able to rent it to the people from Scotland who were renting a flat in Muswell Hill whilst the house sale was going though. They were really nice, quite posh. She wore an Astrakhan coat with a fur collar when she went out, he it seemed, was always in a suit. I can't really remember their names, I think it was something like Irene and Eric, or Ernie, I'm not sure now. I remember that they couldn't have children so they used to spoil me. "Come round whenever you want to," they said. Dad did take me round whenever he was collecting the rent, but there was no chickens there now, they didn't like them, and where the veg was, was now all flowers, it did look very pretty but it wasn't the same. They had even had an inside toilet and bathroom put in, very nice. I wonder if Dad would have done that eventually?

Great excitement in the road. The day of June 2nd 1953 was going to be Coronation day, the crowning of Queen Elizabeth II. Lots of the neighbours got together to make arrangements for the day. Mrs Hammond who lived about four houses down from us said:

"Florrie we are going to rent a fourteen inch screen television, would you and the family like to come and watch the procession? It's in black and white."

"We would like that very much, wouldn't we Margaret? "I don't suppose Wal (my Grandad) will come he's not very royal. I don't know about Tom." Nanna looked at me.

"Of course he'll come, he is royal." He wasn't, but I wasn't going to tell her that.

"Some of the other neighbours are coming." Mrs Hammond said, "I'll make the tea and a sponge cake. Could you make some of your lovely rock cakes?"

"Of course I will," said Nanna. No one knew that it was actually Grandad who made the rock cakes. Nanna looked at me, and just as I was about to say that, she put her finger to her lips. I nodded and we both laughed.

On the day of the coronation, tables were set out in the street, full of good things to eat that all the neighbours had made. It was all covered up with table cloths until after the procession. We all crammed into the Hammond's small living room, us children had the best seat, we sat on the floor cross legged in front of the television. It was the best thing I had ever seen, the golden coach, the Queen in her crown, the beautiful dress, and all her jewels, she really was a real princess.

When it was all over, we all went outside and had a real feast, and a good old sing-song. Dad did come, and I think he enjoyed himself. Someone had a wind-up record player and some Victor Silvester records, so Dad and I had a little waltz together, the next thing we saw was Nanna and Grandad dancing also, I had never seen them dancing before, it was so sweet. By the end of the fifties, nearly everyone, including us, were renting black and white television sets. It was to change everything.

Christmas of 1953 was also a celebration. Firstly, because it was Christmas, secondly it was Dad's birthday on January 1st and it was Nanna's seventieth birthday in February. Grandad decided we would have a big 'shin dig,' as he put it, at Christmas. All the family were roped in to do things. Christmas dinner was just us and a big turkey, so we could have cold cuts in the evening. A few days before he had cooked a rolled piece of beef and a piece of ham. They were stored in the larder. The aunts made sausages on sticks, sausage rolls, trifles, jellies, tinned fruit, and cakes. Nanna had made a lovely Christmas cake and decorated it with the help of Grandad. Dad bought all the drinks; lemonade, ginger beer, and cream soda for us children, beer and spirits for the grown-ups. By the evening the table was laden, everybody who was anybody was invited, from the delivery man who bought our groceries and milk every day, to our closest neighbours and all the families. The parlour had had a spring clean - I had helped with that - a nice big fire was going to air the room.

People were arriving from seven thirty and by eight, the house was full. Us children were tucking into the food and so were the grown-ups, all chatting and drinking, so much noise. Some of us went out into the garden, it was a bit cold, but we slipped our coats on and played ring-o-roses around the apple tree, until we heard music coming from the piano in the parlour. I went in and saw a lot of people singing and dancing, there wasn't much room, but they made do. I took my coat off, underneath I had a new dress, which Dad had bought me. It was white, with pink flowers and green leaves, puff sleeves, and a big gathered skirt, a lace collar and a big net petticoat, I felt the bees-knees.

We sang all the old songs, like '*If You Were the Only Girl in the World.*' I sang '*Why Am I Always a Bridesmaid?*' and everyone joined in. It was great. We finished up with, '*Knees Up, Mother Brown*' and the '*Conga*' which went up and down the stairs, round the living room, out into the back garden, and back into the parlour where everyone collapsed in a heap laughing. Once we all came to, we all sang '*Happy Birthday*' to Nanna. A lot of people with children went home, quite a few sat around talking. Me, I yawned and went to bed. What a lovely day it had been. Mum should have been here. What a time she missed. And we missed her.

Through the 1950's, Nanna's health had got worse. She had what was called then 'a funny turn' (now known as a stroke.) No facial damage, but her walking was very bad. When we took her out it was in a wheelchair. She wasn't very keen but at least it got her out. At this time she just about managed to get upstairs to bed.

One afternoon there was an anxious knock on the door. It was Mrs Witherington from next door to say that her daughter was in a terrible state and she couldn't do anything with her. Her daughter had just had a baby and she couldn't feed her, she hadn't any breast milk. "What am I to do, Mrs Edwards?" Nanna said "Bring the baby in to me. I'll warm up some cows milk, that will settle her down a bit, you get the doctor." So the baby was brought into us. Nanna made up some milk in a little jug, and I held the baby. We wrapped a tea towel around her to keep her arms down, then Nanna fed her with a little spoon. she didn't like it at first, but the poor little mite was so hungry she just took it.

"Keep sitting her up Margaret. Put your hand under her chin and gently rub her back." Nanna said.

"Why do I have to do that?" Looking at her quizzically.

"That brings her wind up. This milk is a bit rich for her really, it might make her a bit sick. She needs baby milk but we haven't got any at the moment. Your dad's gone to the Co-Op on his bike to get some, she's going to need some later on."

"Does that mean we can keep her?" I asked all excited.

"Just for a little while," Nanna laughed, "You just rock her gently and sing her a song and she will go to sleep. I've asked your grandad to clear out one of the drawers from the big chest, put some small blankets in it, and then we will put her in there until her own nanna comes back."

While the baby slept, an ambulance pulled up next door. Men got out, and went into the house. The next minute they were bringing Mrs Witheringtons' daughter out, with a jacket the wrong way round with the sleeves tied behind her back so she couldn't move.

"What are they doing, Nanna? And where are they taking her?"

"I'm sure we will find out soon love," she looked down and smiled.

It wasn't long before Mrs Whitherington came in. She was sobbing. "They have taken her to Claybury, the asylum. They say her breast milk has gone sour and has sent her mad. She needs constant looking after."

Of course, we know now that she had of course got post natal depression. Mrs Witherington took care of her granddaughter all her life. Her mother spent nearly all her life in the asylum, having all sorts of terrible things done to her. She never was fully well again. Everyone in the family did their bit and there was a lot of them. The little girl was very happy, we used to watch her playing in the garden. I will never forget that day when I looked after my first baby.

The Claybury Asylum.

Chapter Five

Coming up to my Eleven Plus exam I had a lot of homework. English wasn't too bad. Because Dad missed out on some of his lessons at school we helped each other. Dad liked to put a bet on now and again, mainly on the flat races, the only jumps he would do was the Grand National. He didn't like the horses getting hurt. In the evening he would say "There's the racing paper, pick me out a winner for tomorrow. Don't forget to look at the runners, riders, and trainers." I would pick the runner I fancied. If it had Lester Piggott, Willie Carson or Pat Eddery riding that was good. Trainers had to be Henry Cecil or Michael Stoute. And if the owner was the Queen, well that was a bonus! Dad won quite a lot when Lester was riding. I had to pick names that Dad could pronounce or he was embarrassed when he went to the bookies.

Once again, if he won a nice lot, I was in for new shoes, or a dress or jumper and skirt, depending on whether it was summer or winter. If it was a really good win, like £100, which it was sometimes, I would get a lovely new coat, which would have to last me quite a few years. It was always too big, so I would grow into it. I wouldn't mind, it was usually pure wool and lovely and warm in the winter.

Sums were a different matter. I was never interested in them, so therefore never good at them. The only way to help with sums was by playing shops, or my post office set. I was the assistant and either Nanna, Grandad, or Dad would be the customer. It worked well until one Sunday afternoon. Nanna was the customer and I was the assistant and we were playing shops. I'd get some groceries out of the cupboard; tins of beans, packets of tea, packets of biscuits, I had put prices on them. Nanna had a shopping bag, she would say what she wanted and I would collect them all together, add them all up, put them in her shopping bag, and she would pay me and I would put the money in the till and work out how much change she would need. It was a good game and I was learning a lot. We had been playing for some time when Nanna said:

"I will have to stop now, I'm getting tired. You are doing really well with your sums," she smiled.

"Oh. Just one more go. Please, Nanna?" I looked at her, I could see she was very pale.

"All right, just one then." She told me what she wanted, I put them in her bag, she gave me the money, but when I went to give her her change she had dropped her bag, and her head had flopped backwards. I called her name and she didn't answer. I was very frightened. What had I done? Grandad was working in the garden, so I ran out to him, calling him.

"Grandad! Come quick! Nanna has fallen asleep and I can't wake her up."

Grandad dropped his fork, came indoors, took one look at Nanna and said to me:

"Don't be frightened. I won't be long. I'm going for the doctor. I think your nan has had another nasty turn. It's not your fault, just stay with her."

"Don't be long!" I shouted, but he was gone. I sat there, it seemed like for hours, just looking at her, hoping she would wake up and we would get on with our game. But she just stayed as still as stone. All of a sudden the back door opened and in came the doctor and Grandad. I ran to him, my arms out.

"Thank goodness!" I said and he put his arms around my shoulders.

"It's all right now. The doctor's here."

The doctor checked her all over, then said to Grandad, "Mrs Edwards has had another stroke. This time it's more severe, she will have to go into hospital for a while to see how much she can do."

I don't know how long Nanna was in hospital for, but I remember that a bed was moved down to the parlour for her, and a piece of furniture was delivered which was put by the side of her bed.

"Nanna's coming home, and she will need us all to look after her. She will be in bed most of the time. We will get her a nice, comfy chair for when she wants to get up. She can't speak much. Grandad will have his work cut out looking after us all, will you help him as much as you can?" Dad said to me.

"Yes Daddy, I'll try." I said, not really knowing what I could do to help.

I was quite shocked when I saw Nanna. She looked quite pale. They brought her indoors in a wheelchair, and put her straight to bed. Once they had got her comfortable, I went up to her and said "I'm so sorry, I made you ill." She didn't say anything. She just looked at me and smiled. I would sit with her when Grandad wanted to go and have a drink with his mates. It was very hard just sitting there with Nanna staring into space. I would sit at the end of her bed and read my book, she would catch my attention if she wanted the commode.

We had got this off to a fine art. I would bring the commode right up next to her, she would lean as far forward as she could I would pull her clothes up at the back and her knickers down. Then as quick as we could I would put my arms under her arms and lift her over to the commode, make sure she didn't wee on her clothes. Then when she was done, do the whole thing in reverse. Once she was comfortable she would grab my hand and hold it tight as if saying thank you. I would laugh and she would just give a big smile, we knew what each other meant. I would go and empty the pot and tears would fall down my cheeks. It must have been very embarrassing for her, bless her.

In 1960 Nanna was taken ill again. She was taken off to hospital, and two days later she died. I wasn't allowed to go to the funeral, so I stayed with Mrs Withington making the tea and sandwiches for when the family came back.

A week or so after Nan died Dad had a visit from someone from the hospital. She told Dad that because Nanna was no longer there to look after me and there was only the two men in the house, that unless a good home was found for me I would have to go into a home, like Barnardos. A children's home.

Dad was furious, "I have been taking care of her since she was five years old, and I still can." "No! I'm sorry, you can't. It's the law," the lady said. Dad sat down in the chair with his head in his hands "Will you give me time to find someone to look after her?" "Yes," she said, "Just let me know when you've done it. I'm really sorry," and she left.

Dad was at his wits end. What was he going to do? He went round to all the aunts on Mums side of the family, but for one reason or another they couldn't take me. He had thought that because they all had children it would be right for me, and that I wouldn't be on my own. The only option left to him was his sister Lol, who had looked after me when I was little and ill. He went round to see her one evening, told her the situation. She hesitated at first, until he almost had to beg and was nearly in tears. Then she agreed. On condition that she had me during the week and then I went to Grandads at the weekend, as they liked to go away to their caravan, and as Jean their daughter was ten years older than me, she would be out a lot of the time.

So an agreement was made. Dad told the hospital, they agreed. Dad told me and I just accepted it. At least I would be staying with dad at weekends. Two weeks later I moved into Broadlands Close, Enfield Highway. I didn't pass my Eleven Plus!

Auntie Lol in her caravan, at Walton-on-the-Naze.

Chapter Six

Broadlands Close was a step up again from Aberdare Road, in as far as it had central heating and a proper bathroom. My room was at the front of the house, 'the box room' they called it, and it was. It consisted of a single bed, a chest of drawers with a mirror on the top, a chair, and at the back of my bed was a fitted cupboard for my clothes and books both reading and writing. I used the chest as a desk to do my homework.

I was at senior school now, and very glad I didn't pass my eleven plus. I liked this school, I was learning quite a lot. My favourite subject was English. The teacher, Mrs Jenkins, was very nice and very helpful, she asked me one day:

"What do you like to do at home Margaret?"

"I like to write stories Miss"

"Alright," she said, "You write me one of your stories and bring it to me the next lesson."

"OK, Miss," I said, and ran all the way back to Aunties to get started.

It was about a mile from school to the Close, the quickest way was through an alleyway, which I didn't like. It was alright in the summer, but in the winter, when the nights were dark it was very creepy. I always thought I was being followed, I was always looking behind me and I ran as fast as I could, I hated that alleyway. I was only twelve. One of the girls from our school got raped in that alley, late at night. She got pregnant as a result and had to leave school. I don't know what happened to her, but it made me even more nervous.

Auntie Lol was a very buxom lady, she used to have her corsets made for her by 'Spirella' I think they were called. Anyway, she had a lady come every so often to measure her up. Because of the corsets, she was very upright and that made her seem very stern, you were almost afraid of her. A very house-proud lady, you had to take your shoes of before you went into the house. I think she thought she was slightly better than the rest of the Edwards family. She married Uncle Jim who was a Clerk of the Works for Enfield Borough Council, which was a middle class occupation. He was a freemason, which was also frowned upon by the family. Most of the Edwards family were working class, and most of the women worked, Auntie Lol didn't. She was a terrible cook and did as little of it as she could. I was glad when I went back to Nanna's at the weekend for some nice food. Grandad did all the cooking, but it was still good.

At senior school we wore a uniform. Really nice; in winter it was a grey pleated skirt, white blouse and red jumper, in summer we wore a red and white dress. In the first year during needlework lessons, we made an apron. The second year we made our own white blouse and in the third year a summer dress. I picked a red and white spotted fabric, all the fabrics were brought into school and you could choose which one you wanted, patterns too. I chose a shirt-waister with flared skirt, cap sleeves and lace collar. I made it under the guidance of Mrs Neal, our needlework teacher who was very clever at her subject, but she did have an unfortunate twitch. She kept hitting her chin on her shoulder, when we first met her we all thought it was very funny and kept copying her, only when she wasn't looking, of course. At one time the whole class was doing it at the same time, we were in fits of laughter, I'm sure she knew, but chose to ignore us. It didn't matter because when we saw the finished garment we were so thrilled with it, we realised how clever the lady was, and we got to like her very much.

The needlework room was a separate building, at the end of the playground, almost next to the wall that divided the juniors from us. It was like a conservatory, bricked a quarter of the way up, then glass and had a pitched roof. Inside there was a row of industrial sewing machines by the side of the windows where we would get the most light. In the middle of the room there was a big table, used for cutting out and watching Mrs Neal teaching.

It was while we were making our dresses one day, that there was a tremendous thunder storm. We had all been working on our sewing machines and Mrs Neal had called us over to the table to show us something, when all of a sudden, a lightning strike came down in between the wall and the room. If we had all been sitting at the machines at the time we would all have been killed. We were very frightened. Everyone was ushered into the main school, some were shaking and we were given a cup of sweet tea and a biscuit. Some went home with their mums, others like me, stayed until the end of the day. I was more concerned about my beautiful dress that I had spent so much time making. As luck would have it, everybody's work was saved, although some were covered in glass but none were cut. The school had to borrow some more machines from another school so we could finish our dresses, and we used the hall instead of the classroom. We were all very proud of our work and wore them all the summer. I think the classroom outside was demolished, just in case it happened again.

The other two outside classrooms were the typing room, and the cookery room. They were proper brick-built buildings, so you felt secure in them. We had to have fluorescent lighting which we weren't used to because the main building had a lot of natural light, but these rooms had no windows, but that was all right. Typing I found very boring, but cooking I liked. When cookery day came around Auntie Lol was pleased as she didn't have to cook. I was pleased because I knew I would get something good to eat. I was quite good at cooking, the only thing I remember was burning the skin of the rice pudding I had made, it didn't matter, because when I got home I just took it off, and the rice inside was delicious. I made savoury and sweet things. I enjoyed cooking.

Auntie Lol took in older students from Enfield College. One of these, Alan, had been lodging with Aunt and Uncle nearly all his student days, so he was more like one of the family. He would either go home to his parents at weekends, or he would go to Jeans (Auntie Lol's daughter, my cousin) for his Sunday dinner. One weekend Auntie Lol and Uncle Jim were going to their caravan, and Jean and her husband Colin were going away too. So Aunt said to me:

"Would you cook Alan's Sunday roast for him?"

"Yes." I said all excited. So Saturday morning I walked into Ponders End to the butchers. I didn't really know what to buy, I went inside and asked the man.

"What do I buy for a Sunday roast please?"

"That would depend on how many you are cooking for," he said.

"Two of us," I said, feeling a bit stupid.

"Well! You could have two legs of a chicken. Half a leg of a lamb. One rib off a cow. Or two pigs trotters," he said, smiling and winking to the other butcher.

"Which is the cheapest?" My aunt hadn't given me very much money.

"The pigs trotters are the cheapest," he said, more seriously, "But they don't really make a good roast. I suggest you have the chicken legs. Who's cooking this roast?"

"I am," I replied confidently, "I know how to do it, I learnt it at school."

"Good for you, young lady. Can we come?" he said, still grinning.

"Sorry, there ain't enough. Bye!" I said, walking out of the shop.

"Don't burn yourself!" he shouted after me.

I waved, and moved on to the greengrocers, to get the vegetables. I had to think what veg I had done at school. Carrots, that's what we'll have.

"Can I help you, miss?" The greengrocer asked.

"I would like two carrots, please," I said, letting him see that I knew what I was talking about.

"Right, two pounds of carrots," he said and started putting lots of carrots in a paper bag.

"No!" I cried. "I only want two carrots." He tipped all the carrots out of the bag.

"You're pushing the boat out today," he moaned, "Tuppence please."

"Oh! And two potatoes. Large ones," I said. He put them in the bag, tutting. I paid and left the shop quickly. I walked home singing. This was better than playing pretend shops at Nanna's.

The cooking went well.

"This is the best meal I have ever eaten," Alan said.

I was thrilled! It was nice I have to say. For afters, Alan opened a tin of peaches, and we found some ice cream in the little freezer, a real treat. I was so proud of myself for being so independent. Alan washed up, he was a real gent and like a big brother. I went upstairs and wrote this as my story for school the next day.

In the Summer, when I came home from school, Aunt and I would sit in the garden, she in the old deckchair and me on the grass. There was a girl next door a little bit older than me, and she was swinging on her swing. I had never spoken to her since I had lived there. I was envious of her on her swing. I got up off the ground and went to the fence.

"Hello!" I shouted, "Do you live here? What's your name?"

"Hello. Yes I do live here, and my name is Iris. Are you living with Mrs Weeks?"

"Yes," I said, "She's my aunt."

"Oh!" She said, still swinging. "Would you like to come round and play on my swing?"

I looked at Aunt and smiled, she smiled back.

"Can I go?" I asked politely.

"Course you can," she said, pleased that I had made a friend.

"I'm coming round now!" I shouted, all excited. Iris jumped off the swing and came and met me at the door. She introduced me to her mum, and we both went into the garden. She pushed me on the swing, I waved to Aunt, she waved back.

Iris had a piano and had lessons once or twice a week. The teacher came to her home, and what she taught Iris, Iris then taught me. I could only ever play with my right hand, but I could play tunes like 'O, Come All Ye Faithful,' and 'A Nightingale Sang in Berkley Square.' I loved that song. So when Iris was having her piano lesson, I would go out on the swing, swinging as high as I could, singing at the top of my voice:

That certain night, the night we met
there was magic abroad in the air,
There were angels dining at the Ritz
and a nightingale sang in Berkley Square.

I maybe right and I maybe wrong,
But I'm perfectly willing to swear,
But when you'd turned and smiled at me,
A nightingale sang in Berkley Square

The moon that lingered over London Town,
Poor puzzled moon, he wore a frown,
How could he know we two were so in love,

As the song got louder and louder, I made the swing go higher and higher.

The whole darn world was upside down.

The streets of town, were paved with stars
It was such a romantic affair,
And as we kissed and said goodnight,
A nightingale sang in Berkley Square.

The swing started slowing down.

I know 'cause I was there,
That night in Berkley Square.

The version I liked the best was sung by Vera Lynn. The piano teacher said "Who is that singing?" "That's my friend next door, she's always singing on the swing." "She should have some singing lessons," the teacher said with interest, "She has a really nice voice." "I'll tell her that, she will be pleased," Iris said. And I was.

Instead of singing lessons, I took up tap and ballet dancing classes. They were run by a little short lady, I only ever knew her as Lillian. The lessons were held in a little hall in Enfield. There were about twelve of us, all shapes and sizes and we all got on pretty well as I recall. The ones I remember were Maureen, my namesake Margaret and Diane. She and I became best friends. I used to go to her house and practice for the shows.

An Oriental number. I am third from the right

Ballet classes, I am in front, on the far right, kneeling.
My friend Diane is second right on the back row

They had an open fire and had a trivet but with longer legs, on which a kettle stood, and it was always nearly boiling. Anyway, one day, Diane's mum had just popped out to see a friend and we were just practising a ballet routine, when Diane kicked the kettle of boiling water all over her ankle. She screamed. I ran out into the kitchen and poured some vinegar onto a clean cloth and wrapped it around her ankle, then rang for an ambulance. When the ambulance arrived, they looked at her ankle and said "Who put this cloth on your ankle?" I looked worried, I'd thought I'd done something wrong. Diane said "My friend did." The ambulance man looked at me and said "Was that you?" I said "Yes" sheepishly. "Well done. You have done well, she won't have such a bad scar now," and she didn't.

One day I came home from school and was told by Aunt that Iris and her family were moving to Rayleigh in Essex. We never kept in touch.

In 1957 Auntie Florrie and her family moved to Walton-on-the-Naze, Essex and started doing bed and breakfast, just like Auntie Win who we used to stay with. We swapped our holidays to Auntie Florrie's, were Dad could sleep in a caravan instead of a garage. I slept in the conservatory with my cousins Pam and Sue, who were nearer my age.

Dad and I still had just two weeks holiday which was never enough for me. So at the age of fourteen Aunt Flo asked me if I would like to spend the school holidays with them, helping with the breakfasts.

"Yes! Yes! Yes please!" I said.

"It does mean that you will have to travel one way on the coach on your own," she told me.

A photo of a mid 1950's coach

That was the down-side, but I was determined to do it. So from 1960, Dad and I would travel to Walton together, Dad would stay for two weeks as usual, and then he would go home and back to work. I would stay at Aunts for the rest of the holidays. It was hard work but great fun. Sue, Pam and I slept in the conservatory which was quite hot and quite frightening when we had a big thunder storm in the night. I would scream, dive under the covers and cry. Pam would say, "Come on Margaret, don't be a big baby. It's not going to hurt you." I think I still had the memories of the school needlework room.

The routine would be: up in the morning, have some cornflakes, then get ready to take the first tray - which was the heaviest. It would depend on what room you were taking it to. The house had one room with two single beds, one room with one double and one single bed, one family room, which had a double bed two single beds and a cot The last room had a double bed, a single bed and a cot. Each room also had a table and the relevant number of chairs. So the trays got heavier the bigger the room. The tray contained teapot, hot water jug, milk jug, sugar basin, cups, saucers, cereals and dishes, plates, knives, forks, and spoons, toast and toast rack, and a pot of jam. It was amazing that very little got broken. The second tray had to be taken up very quickly and carefully, as it was the main breakfast. Most mornings it was egg, bacon, tomatoes, mushrooms, sausage, and dippy, which was fried bread but not fried, grilled, usually spread with dripping, it was delicious. It all had to be taken up quickly so as not to get cold. On Fridays they had smoked haddock and a poached egg, with bread and butter, one of my favourite breakfasts.

Once the breakfasts were done, we had the rest of the day to ourselves, and we used to like to go to the pier. Our uncle was in charge of the speedway, so we got in for free. We were never allowed to wear make-up, Uncle Wal never approved, so we put it all in our handbags and we'd put it on across the road, on the green. We went to the pier, had some fun and then rubbed the make-up off on the way home! I never really knew whether Auntie Florrie knew what we did, I suspect she did, but she never said anything, we just couldn't stop giggling. Work to be done before bed; trays to be laid out for breakfasts the next day, then cocoa and bed, another long day tomorrow.

Saturdays were change-over day. Beds to change, rooms to clean, in fact the whole house had to be cleaned. With no time for cooking, we would stop at one o'clock and one of us would go down to the fish shop at the end of the road to get fish and chips and a Lyons individual apple pie. Oh my, what a treat! It never touched the sides we were so hungry, we never really minded how much work we did on a Saturday. We always looked forward to our fish and chips, new guests, and if we were very lucky tips. They were good days. Auntie Flo had a lovely cocker spaniel called Trudie and in the year of 1960 she had a litter of little black and white puppies. My dad loved them and he wanted to take one home, but he said it wasn't fair as he was at work all day and Grandad was too old to look after a puppy, so we made the most of playing with them while we were on holiday.

Back at Broadlands Close, friends were few and far between. I had one friend who was also a neighbour, well in the next road. I can't really remember how we became friends, but her and her family kept me sane, many times. I had lots of happy holidays in the caravan with Jill. Also many happy Christmases with them. Her name was Jillian Evans. Her mum was a little lady, very sweet, her dad was Welsh, a postman, and tall and thin with a cheeky grin. Her grandmother lived with them and she was lovely too. I didn't know their proper names, I always called them Mum, Dad, and, Gran, and they were my real family for a long time. They asked me at one time if I would like to go to a holiday camp with them.

This was the first real holiday I had ever had. I had to ask permission first, but Aunt said yes, so off we went. I can't remember how we got there, but I think by train. All the Evans family came plus Jill's Auntie Peggy who was also great fun. The holiday camp was a small family run one and Jill and I had a chalet to ourselves. There was lots of things to do, a nice beach, the food was good, and we went in the sea every day. On the last day of the holiday there was a fancy dress competition and Mum Evans suggested I went as a hula-hula girl. So we all spent the day on the beach, making a grass skirt, covering a bra with leaves made of crepe paper and a head-band. It looked great. The competition was in the evening, and guess what? I won first prize, I can't remember what the prize was, I was only interested in the cheeky remark Ken the green coat said, "I award the first prize to Margaret for the stunning costume, although I did think she was a lot slimmer than she is. Only joking!" I did get a cuddle from him though before we left to come home. That was a really lovely holiday.

Photos on the next page: The Evans family. My prize-winning costume. Sunbathing. Ken, the cheeky Greencoat.

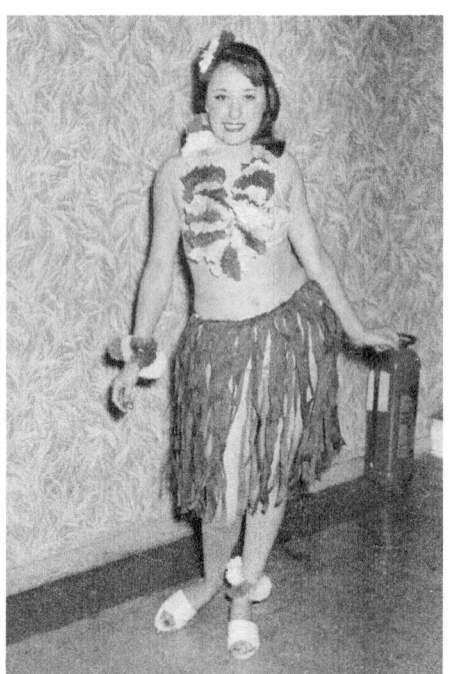

Tap and ballet classes went by the board when boys came on the scene. Boyfriend number one was Ian. Whenever we went out on a date he would ask if he could bring his bike, as he didn't like walking home in the dark. He was a real sweetie! We only ever went walking, neither of us had very much money, he always made sure I was home by ten o'clock, which was the time Aunt wanted me in by. A quick kiss goodnight and off he would go on his bike.

Every boyfriend I had was treated to a holiday at Walton. There was a good reason for that. They had to be vetted by Aunt Florrie. She was a good judge of character. If she said she liked them then I would stay with them until the next one came along, which is what happened to Ian.

I remember one Sunday we had gone for a walk as usual, Ian asked me back to his house for a cup of tea and to meet his mum, I said I would like that. We were walking up the path when he stopped short. He had a broken mudguard on his bike, and the end of it was in my knee before I knew it, my leg was pouring with blood. I'm not good with blood. I shouted to Ian to get his mum, and that I was going to pass out. He yelled at his mum and she came running, took me inside, sat me in the chair and then I was gone, out like a light.

When I came to my leg was dressed with a bandage and a hot cup of tea with two sugars, a drop of brandy in it, was there on the table. That went down very well. I had never had alcohol before. Ian's mum was very nice. I thanked her for everything then very gingerly, Ian, me, and the wretched bike walked home. That was the last time I saw Ian. I think he may have felt guilty. And for me it was time to move on to boyfriend number two. Ian and I were friends for nearly two years, but it had run its course.

Dave was a near-disaster. An octopus! Hands all over my body, I kneed him in the groin, headed for the front door and made for home. The next day I felt very shaky, and looked in the mirror, and saw a horrible mark on my neck, a so-called 'love bite', but no love was involved. It taught me a lesson. Always be careful who you date. I wore a high neck sweater for a few days to hide the mark in case anyone should ask questions, which thank goodness they didn't.

Jill had a boyfriend too. Charlie. A really nice guy, he thought the world of Jill, so I never felt guilty about having boyfriends, and we had begun to lose touch anyway.

1961 and I was a working girl at Boots the Chemists. I loved it. I made lots of friends both boys and girls, although my main friend was Joan. She helped me get to grips with the job. The others I got on really well with where, Lannie, a really bright spark, full of fun. Sylvia, an older lady - the mothering kind - was always there to give help and advice; and Brenda who was quiet and shy, but she had style. We all worked very well together. I was working in the dispensary, counting tablets, mixing lotions. I really enjoyed every minute of it. Mr Neal, was the manager and he asked me one day if I would like to be a pharmacist.

"Yes sir," I said, eagerly.

"OK. I will look into it."

Two weeks or so went by and then Mr Neal called me into his office. He said that I could do it if I did five years at college with one day working at Boots and then five years learning Latin. My face dropped.

"Thank you sir, can I think about it?" I asked.

"Of course you can," said Mr Neal.

I did and I turned it down. I didn't mind the first bit, but the thought of doing five years learning Latin filled me with dread. I went back to doing my job but now my heart wasn't in it.

The next boyfriend was Colin. I met him at Walton while he

was visiting his grandmother. He was very tall, very handsome, and he knew it! He came to Aunts, to tea, and when he went home I said to her as I always did:

"Well what do you think?"

She looked at me.

"Hmm. I think he's a nit-wit with a big head!" We all agreed and laughed, hence Colin was no more.

Christopher was a Mod with a scooter. I am five foot tall, and he was shorter than me which was very odd. We met at the Tottenham Royal ballroom. Jill and I used to go there when we could afford it. It was very plush, with draped curtains, red velvet seats, a live band, and good dancers. Chris was one of them. I really enjoyed ballroom dancing. Jill and Charlie got the bus home while Chris ran me home on the back of his scooter. He often came to tea at Grandad's. We went out together for about five months, which up to then is the longest I'd been out with anyone. I don't know why I gave him up, I think it was because along came Reg and I decided I would rather be a Rocker than a Mod.

Tottenham Royal, in the mid 1960's

Chapter Seven

In 1962 I was 17 years old. I was still working for Boots, having fun, going to parties, meeting new friends, enjoying my work. Every now and again a boy would come into the shop all dressed in black leather, wearing a crash helmet, ask for something we didn't have, then walk out again. We were starting to get a bit suspicious, and were about to ask him what he was playing at. I was on my own on the counter, he could see that, he took off his helmet, blushed and asked me if I would like to have a coffee with him.

"Yes I would. But I'm not going on no motorbike with this tight skirt on," I said.

"OK. If I can leave my crash hat here, we can walk to the coffee bar from here," the boy said.

That started a two year love affair, which was great fun. He lived locally and had a big family, one of which no one ever talked about – Billy, who it turned out, spent a time in prison – did I want to know? No. When I met him, he seemed very nice.

Reg was the leather-clad boy's name, and motorbikes were his game. He lived and breathed them, and so did his friend Jim, and we became close friends too, although he looked and smelt like a grease monkey, he had a heart of gold. So did Reg's mum. We became very close, although they never knew my history, and I never wanted to talk about it.

Left: Reg, in his leathers. Right: Me and Jim, Reg's grease-monkey friend

We did go down to Walton on the bike. I needed to know what Auntie Florrie thought of him of course! I was quite surprised when she said she did like him. They got on like a house on fire. We went to Walton a lot.

Christmases were spent either with Reg's mum and dad, again I never knew her name, (I only ever called her 'Mum') or with Reg's sister, Peggy. Great, silly and fun Christmases they were too. I never missed being at home at all. Where was home anyway?

Nearly two years being friends, and Reg decided to move things on. He knew I wouldn't be happy with that. It was made clear by me right from the start that no sex was going to happen. I had seen too many of the girls at school ruin their lives by getting pregnant or having abortions. Contraception was not that good at this time, so until I was married and settled, I was having none of it!

One day Jim told me that Reg had been seeing someone else. It turns out it had been going on for sometime, probably for sex, who knows? I confronted him, and he admitted he was seeing someone else, so that was that. It ended. If that's what he wanted, I felt he couldn't have thought that much of me. I was upset, I thought maybe he was the one I would marry.

Life wasn't good at that time. I was falling out with Auntie Lol, and I spent a lot of time with Auntie May, her sister. She had also fallen out with Lol, because of me. Auntie Lol thought she was taking me away from her.

As it happened, my cousin Miriam was preparing to get married and had asked me to be her bridesmaid. I said yes, thinking maybe we were friends again. How wrong could I be? With her going, they had a room for me to move into with them, but it would mean me having to pay rent.

Brenda, with her long legs and her Vauxhall Cresta car

At work, we had a new girl start called Brenda. We hit it off straight away and we became friends. She was bored with Boots, and I needed to earn more money as I had moved in with Auntie May. Brenda had found a job with British Rail as a punch operator.

"What's that? I can't do that," I said to her.

"They train you," she replied.

"OK." I said. So we both gave a weeks notice. I was sad to leave Boots, I enjoyed the work, but the money was not enough and I didn't want the chance of meeting up with Reg again. I was just about getting over him.

Well. It was quite an exciting time working for BR. I had never worked in an office before. We were in a room full of girls, all punching away on little machines making holes in cards. We were paying the worker's wages. When we had finished with our cards they would go to be checked by the supervisor, if they were wrong they came back to you, if they were right, they went straight into a big machine, (an early type of computer) and made ready for the wages to be paid out. I liked the work. When I first started there I was getting a lot of rejects, but as time went on I was getting better. I didn't like sitting down all day, I wasn't used to it, but the money was better than Boots so I put up with it.

Hand-operated card punch. Exactly the type I used at British Rail

I still went to the coffee bar to see the people I knew there, I wouldn't call them friends because most of them were prostitutes. I thought maybe I would see Reg there, but I never did.

My life changed again. Welcome to 'bed-sit land'. I needed to find a flat or bedsit, where I could get a bus to work.

I don't know how I found the attic bedsit, in a big, old house. It was very creepy. I think I must have been desperate, or it was cheap, probably the latter. It was furnished, with a single bed, a wash-basin (with just cold water), a small table-top cooker, electric - so the kettle took forever to boil. Of course that was the idea, the meter ate the coins. I used to have to keep the curtains closed in the mornings, while I washed in cold water, because the dirty old landlord would stand at the garden gate and look up at the window, hoping to see me washing myself, that's why it was put there I suspect. However, it was nice and easy to get the bus, the 6.00am, which took me straight to BR.

I was thinking of changing jobs again. I didn't think I would earn enough to pay my bills there (BR), but I would stay where I was until I found somewhere else to work, and as it happened that came sooner than I thought.

We often used to celebrate the birthdays of the office girls in some way, sometimes it was cakes, sometimes we would all go to the pub, as it was on this day. When lunch time came, off we trotted to the nearby pub, I think there were quite a few of us. On these occasions I never knew what to drink. I didn't drink alcohol usually, so being undecided, I asked my friend what she was drinking. "It's barley wine. It's like a strong beer, try some." I had heard of barley wine, it was a beer that my nan used to put into the Christmas puddings. Anyway, I tried some of hers, and it was really nice. Yes, I will have one of those. Well, one led to two, and possibly three... Who knows? I only know that when the air hit me when I came out of the pub I couldn't stand up. The girls had to help walk me back to work! Of course, the supervisor called me into the office...

"You're drunk," she stated.

"Yes," I said, holding on to the back of the chair, so as not to fall over.

"I think I will have to sack you. Your work hasn't been up to scratch anyway lately. I have been finding a lot of mistakes in the cards. You have been paying the railwaymen a lot of extra money."

"I expect they've earned it." I was getting bored with job anyway.

"I will give you a weeks notice," she said and I staggered out of the room.

I would never have talked to anyone like that if I hadn't been drunk. The other girls were mortified, "Shall we go and explain?" "No," I said, "I was thinking of leaving anyway!"

What am I going to do now? I had a week to find another job. Which I did, in a factory. From 7.30am until 5.00pm, with an hour for lunch. It was the most boring job ever, but the money was good, £70 per week, and that was a good wage in the 1960's.

I still kept in touch with the girls at Boots; Joan, my best friend asked me what I did at the weekend, I told her nothing much. She said that her and Vince, her fiancé, ran the cloakroom at the Wood Green Jazz Club and would I like to go on Saturday? I said yes. I had never really liked traditional jazz, but it was very popular in the mid-sixties.

So with a tight mini-dress on, and face made-up, we were off. I had never been to a jazz club before. The only place I had danced before was at the Tottenham Royal, ballroom dancing, with Jill and I had loved it. This was slightly different, you listened to the bands, there wasn't much room to dance. With bands like

Kenny Ball & his Jazzmen, Aker Bilk & the Paramount Jazz Band, Chris Barber, and the resident *Alex Welsh Band*. Yes, I am name dropping! I used to drink in the bar with all of them at different times. Oh, and not forgetting dear old *Humphrey Lyttleton*. I was introduced to the couple who ran the club, Art and Viv Sanders and a guy called John who was a sort of caretaker-cum-bouncer. He knew Joan and Vince, and they told everyone that I was there to help, so I got in for free. I did help and I did enjoy it. Every weekend I would now go to the jazz club. One evening Joan asked me if I would let John run me home. I had got to know him quite well, so I said yes. I had forgotten that he rode a motorbike, and that I had another very short, tight, mini-dress on. "Never mind, he said just hoist it up and jump on!" We started going out from then on.

I was still living in that horrible bedsit, two things happened while I was there which made me think that I should move on. Every Friday after work I would go and spend an hour with Dad and Grandad before I went home on the bus. This particular night I caught the bus as usual, got off at the end of the road and started walking home. It was a long road and very dark. Halfway down I knew there was someone behind me. I tried not to take any notice, but started walking faster, and so did he, then from the back he grabbed me. I screamed and whacked him with my handbag, and ran all the rest of the way home. When I got there, Joan and Vince were waiting at the doorstep. I burst into tears and told them what had happened, Vince flew down the stairs to see if he could see anyone, but whoever it was had gone.

The second thing that happened was that I was on my way to work. I used to have to catch the 5.30am bus to get to work by 6.00am, that was the time the paper boys would deliver the papers on their bikes. One morning I was walking to catch the bus, when this paper boy crossed to where I was walking. As he passed me, his flies were open and his penis was erect. I was so shocked! I ran all the way to the bus. Sitting on the bus, I thought "I have had enough of this!" So, at the police station, I got off the bus and went in. I knew I was going to be late for work but I didn't care, he can't get away with it. If he does that to me, what will he do to someone else? I told the police everything and they agreed with me. They asked me did I think he would still be there? I said yes. OK, they said, jump in the car and lets see if we can find him.

So here I was haring around the streets of North London in a police car, then all of a sudden I spotted him.

"There he is!" I shouted.

"Right," said the policeman, "You stay here and we will call out another car to take him in."

When we got back to the station they asked me did I want to press charges.

"No," I said, "I just want him to have a warning, that's all. I've got to get back to work, I'm late."

"Oh, he's had a warning, all right. We have scared him half to death, he says he will never do it again, and don't you worry about getting to work, we will take you," he said kindly.

So there I was driving though the gates of the factory, looking very embarrassed. The gatekeeper, who I knew and used to speak to every morning, stopped the car and said to me:

"Goodness me, what have you done?"

"She's done nothing wrong. She's been helping with our inquires," the policeman said.

"All right, have you clocked in yet?"

"No," I replied.

"Well, don't worry about that, I'll see to it." And he did. I didn't get into any trouble.

This was the first time I'd thought, where was my mum when I needed her? Where was she? Was she alive or dead? Why hasn't she been in touch? I had kept in touch with all the family and no-one had heard from her. It had occurred to me, every girl and boyfriend had had a mum I was close to. I had had many mums and they were lovely, even John's mum was nice. I had been going round nearly every Sunday to lunch, but none of them were *my* mum. I was on my own.

I hated the bed-sit I was in. John and I agreed that it would be better if I moved to Wood Green. Apart from seeing my Dad there was nothing keeping me in Enfield, so having given a weeks notice to both the landlord and my employer, I packed up what things I had and moved to Wood Green, the start of a new life for me.

The bed-sit I moved into was so much better than the one in Enfield. For a start it was on the High Street, so no dark roads to walk down. It was a big house, with three floors. The ground floor was rented by a family; the mother was disabled, the father was retired, and they had a little girl of about six years old. On the next floor, straight in front of the stairs, was a 70 year-old lady who - I found out later - had come home from Australia, where she had been living with her daughter, but it was far too hot out there for her. My room was next.

It was quite nice, it wasn't very big, a chest, shelves fitted into the recess, with the meter in the cupboard underneath, - which I seemed to be constantly feeding - a small electric fire, a single bed, with a candlewick bedspread and a big window looking out onto the garden. There was a small kitchen area in the corner, a table and two chairs along the wall, the bathroom and toilet were on the landing between Julie, (the elderly lady) and me. The rent was £25 a week, which was about right for the mid to late sixties.

The electric was very expensive. I used to put half my wages for the electric in a tin, but in the winter it was never enough. I would have to go cold or John would have to give me some money to put in until I got paid again.

I got a job in the local chemist. Shop work wasn't well paid, but I loved it, and I didn't want to go back to office or factory work. The manageress was a lovely Jewish lady, very helpful and very kind, she knew I lived on my own in a bedsit. She was always bringing me in some of their own food that was left over from the weekend, which I was very grateful for. There was never very much money left over for food for the week. I would go to Johns parents for Sunday lunch, always a roast of some sort, and I always had seconds, then a pudding. I was always stuffed afterwards and it was either a walk, or a sleep in the chair. Going back to Mrs Jacks, my manageress, and how kind she was: I remember one really cold winter, a lot of people had gone down with 'flu, including me. There were no telephones, no way of contacting her, and I couldn't get out of bed. Suddenly about 7.00pm, a knock came at my door. I managed to get to the door, and it was Mrs Jacks. Huddled in a tea-towel was a big bowl of hot, chicken soup.

"There you are, my dear. I thought you might have the 'flu when you didn't show up for work today. You take however long you need to get better, this might help."

"Oh! Thank you so much. I haven't felt like eating anything all day." That was the best soup I had ever tasted. It lasted me for two days. I felt much better and went back to work the following week. Even now when I'm feeling unwell, that's the first thing I have is a big bowl of chicken soup, it works every time.

Holidays were spent at Walton with Auntie Florrie. She was still doing bed and breakfast. Bill and Helena, John's parents would spend their two week holiday with us there. When the weather was good we would take my cousin's daughter Angie, she was about three, down to the beach and play with the ball or build sand castles. It was a fun time then, just laying in the sun, you could be anywhere in the world. One morning Bill got up and came downstairs to go to the outside lav, we were not up and the upstairs toilet was busy. Quite a while passed. Aunt was in the kitchen making breakfast, when she said "What's that noise?" It stopped, and she carried on working. Helena came down, "Where's Bill?" she said. "I expect he's gone for a walk," sometimes he did that. Then all of a sudden Aunt said "There's that noise again." We all stopped what we were doing and listened. It was a voice calling from outside. We all went to see. It was Bill. Someone had locked the door of the lav, I think it might have been Uncle wandering around the garden, as he did in the morning. We all laughed, he saw the funny side too. For years afterwards, we all sang:

Oh dear, what can the matter be?
Bill got locked in the lavatory.
He was there from Monday to Saturday,
Nobody knew he was there.

Angie and Me playing ball at Hipkins Beach, Walton-on-the-Naze

On my 21st birthday

On the 21st of October, 1966 I was 21 years old. We didn't make a big thing of it, I was still living in the bedsit. We just had a few friends round; Joan and Vince, Barry and Barbara, Denise and her boyfriend, I can't remember his name. They were all good friends at the time, but like most people, you lose touch, don't you – apart from Joan and Vince – who now live near by.

From left to right: Joan, Vince, John, Barry and a question mark!

At Christmas that year, we were spending the day at John's auntie Win's. All the family were there, sitting round the dinner table, when out of the blue John produced a ring and asked me to marry him. Of course I said yes!

In 1968, John and I were married at St. Marks' church, Wood Green, on a damp and dreary day in January. I was warm, dressed in a heavy brocade dress with a fur collar and cuffs, with fur pill-box hat, and a short veil. When we came out of the church, I was convinced Mum would be standing there, waiting for me. No one was there. For a little while I was upset and disappointed, but when I saw all her family, and mine had turned up, I was thrilled to see them all, and it made up for her not being there.

So after nearly five years of living on my own and being independent, I now had a husband and family to look after me, and they did for many years.

John and I were married on 27th January 1968.
On the left is Dads family. On the right is Mums family.
There is one person missing...

Chapter Eight

Our married life started with us living with John's parents, this was while John made the upstairs into a flat. We slept on an old iron bedstead which creaked and squeaked every time you moved, which made us giggle every time we tried to have a cuddle. Knowing his mum and dad were next door it was quite embarrassing! We also had to live with gas lighting which in 1968 was unusual, but the old lady who lived there before wouldn't have any work done, of any sort, so that was one of the first things we had done, electricity.

Once we were settled in the flat, we decorated it in 1970's style, three walls were orange and the chimney breast was chocolate brown. It sounds awful now, but we thought we were very modern. The furniture we were proud of. There were the two bucket chairs, in black with bright orange seats, not very comfortable, but looked good.

John was working as a proofreader in London and I was working part-time in the chemist just around the corner. It was just a small shop, which I loved, really nice people, the wages weren't that good but I didn't have rent to pay and it was a job I liked doing.

Elsie (I think) and Mr Richardson, the pharmacist

Our honeymoon was more of a holiday, because we were married in the January and the holiday itself was in the August and it was with friends of ours. We went to Dawlish in Dorset and stayed in a chalet, surrounded by trees and bushes. Inside we had to do a spider catching exercise before we could sleep, there were hundreds of them. I was pleased when we came home, I hated spiders.

Talking about insects, while we were living at the flat, John was working night work. I had just got into bed when I could hear a rustling by the bed. I knew Helena and Bill were sleeping below me in the downstairs bedroom and I didn't want to disturb them, so I laid there waiting to hear the sound again. Nothing. I turned over to go to sleep, when all of a sudden there was a huge rustling coming from the waste paper basket by the bed. Oh, my goodness! I thought, it's a mouse. I don't like them either. It went quiet, so I crept downstairs and tapped on Helena's door, I think she had heard something anyway. We crept upstairs, me behind her, I was not going first. We went into the bedroom, me still behind her, we heard nothing until she touched the bag that was in the bin, then we heard it. I screamed! Mum grabbed the bag and we both headed for the front door, where Mum opened the bag. We both thought out would come a mouse, but no. It was the biggest beetle I have ever seen! Even Mum jumped when it came out onto the garden. I didn't sleep for days and John thought it was very funny. Hmm... And Bill slept through it all.

Life went on. I had changed my job again and was now working at a bakers, just part-time, but with slightly more money. We were saving as much as we could so we could get a mortgage on a house of our own. We had been in the flat for nearly two years, and everyone kept asking when are we going to have children. Not yet, when we have a house of our own, we used to say. Right! So what happened? I fell pregnant. Everybody was really pleased, including us.

The one person I wanted to tell, but couldn't, was my mum. Still no-one knew where she was. Some of the family thought she might be living in Ireland, I think one of the family tried the Salvation Army (who used to help trace missing persons) but with no success. We just thought that maybe she would get in touch when she was ready.

I was still in touch with her family, mostly her sister, my aunt Mary. We used to go to the auctions with her and her daughter, my cousin, Barbara. We would buy what was called a 'box of useful oddments.' We would bid for the whole box and would get it for £1. We would then drive back to Auntie Mary's for a cup of tea and a piece of bread and home-made raspberry jam, and a look at what goodies we had in our boxes. We did very well most of the time, things we could clean up and sell at the local car boot sale. Such fun!

Our beach hut, at Hipkins Beach, Walton-on-the-Naze

It was on one of these trips out when Auntie Mary mentioned to me about a beach hut up for sale, very near to hers at Walton-on-the-Naze, and would we be interested? I knew where they were and straight away said 'yes.' I spoke to John, and he said it would depend on how much it was. We went to see it and spoke to the owner, who could see I was well into my pregnancy, and was highly delighted about a family having the hut, and so lowered the price. We took it over straight away.

There were two ways of getting to the hut, one was down a steep slope and the other was steep steps. I chose the steep steps, because the other way I was at risk of taking a tumble. As it was, it was a good job the steps had a hand rail, I had to come down side ways as I couldn't see my feet, one step at a time.

Well! Did we get a shock when we opened the door. There was a boat inside! Not a small boat, but one that took up the whole hut. We got someone to help get it out, and underneath there must have been about three or four inches of sand under the mats. It took some clearing out, I can tell you.

On the 8th of August 1970, our daughter was born. I couldn't wait to get home. Me and insects just don't go. The hospital was overrun with cockroaches.

"Don't leave your slippers on the floor. Tuck the babie's blankets up onto the cot, and tuck your blankets under the mattress," the nurse would say.

If you walked down the corridor you squelched them as you trod on them.

"Can I go home yet?" I asked the nurse.

"Not yet, you have no milk to feed her."

"Are you surprised? In this horrible place! No fresh air, bars at the windows, and pests wherever you look."

"Get me out of here," I said to John one day when he came to visit, "I will feed her much better at home."

I came home one day sooner than I was supposed to although I was still in that place for a week, it was good to be home.

Melanie Helena Herbert, born 8th August, 1970

"What shall we call her?" John asked one day.

"I don't know. What about Helena after your mother?" We were watching television at the time and an advert came on with a little girl asking her mummy for a glass of Lucozade. '*Of course you can Melanie.*'

"That's it!" said John, "I like that name."

So all the next day we were going round the house saying 'Melanie Herbert', to see if the first name would go with the second. It did. I still wanted to keep Helena in there somewhere, so she was called Melanie Helena Herbert, which was a mouthful, and still is.

John was working on a veg stall on a Saturday for a friend. There suddenly was a knock on the door, and when I answered it there stood John with a little fluffy thing inside his coat. It was an eight week old, mongrel puppy. John said a neighbour had walked past the stall with it on the way to the pet shop because no-one wanted it. He thought he would come and ask if we could take him. He knew he didn't have to ask really. He was ours straight away and we called him Bobby.

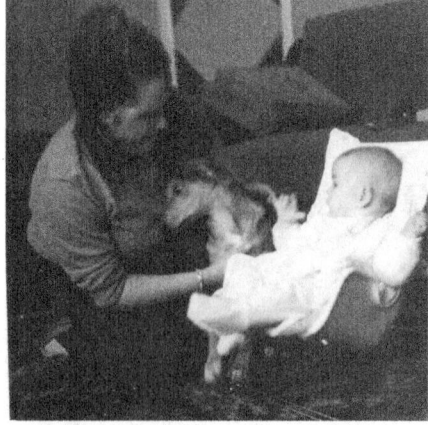

Bobby and Mel became great friends

Bobby and Mel were great friends, even to the point that when she was crawling she would make her way to the kitchen, pick out all the dog biscuits, eat all the charcoal ones and crawl back into the living room with a very black face. They never seemed to do her any harm. He used to sleep under her hand when she was in the relax-a-chair.

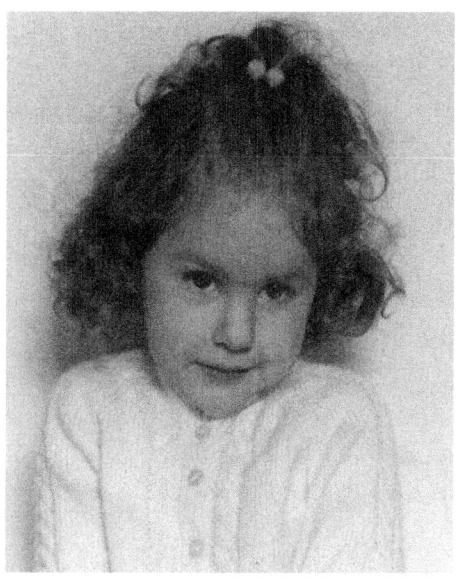

Mel, aged about two or three

Mel, as she is known now, was two years old when we moved to our first house. A terraced house in a quiet street, walking distance to the shops and a market which we would go to and do our shopping, where Mel would get lost. Often coming back on some policeman's shoulders...

"Does this little girl belong to you," the policeman would ask.

"Oh! Yes thank you officer. Where did you find her?"

"She was just sitting in the middle of the field. So I thought I had better take her before someone else does. She's been sitting in the police station playing with the toys that we keep for lost children."

"Thank you! We will keep an eye on her in future"

Well, that didn't work. The next time she got lost, we found her sitting in the centre of the Co-Op toy department, playing with the toys. We said to the staff "Why didn't you put it across the Tannoy?" "She was having such a lovely time, we didn't want to disturb her!" Aargh! Time to get some reins I think.

John had changed his job. He was now working for the newspapers and it was mainly shift work. He decided that in the winter he would work double shifts, so we could have the summers down at the beach hut. Which was great in the summer, but made the winters very long. I was only just learning to drive, so had no real independence.

I had two bouts - if that's what you want to call them - of post-natal depression, one of which was after a very bad attack of chicken pox. I was laid up for three weeks and the doctor was in to see me every day.

I think the depression was partly to do with the fact that you always need your mum when your not well, and so I felt it was time once again to try and find her. I got in touch with Auntie Mary to see if she had any news or had had any letters from her. She gave me a letter she had had from Mum soon after she had left. She was asking if the divorce had come though as she wanted to re-marry.

The letter had no address, just a post office box number. Sylvie didn't want any one to know where she was and Auntie was to promise to keep it a secret. It talked about how good Oxford was, how she would have loved to bring me there, but Jack would never agree to it.

I've included a copy of the letter on the next page. As you can see the address has been torn off and it ends rather abruptly.

Top: Dad, Jonathon (from the next-door hut), Me, Auntie Mary, my cousin David
Below: Auntie Mary and Auntie Win on holiday in later years

1952

Dear Mary,

Just a few lines thanking you for your letter & all the news, my how the time does go by, honestly when you think of Barbara getting married & Brian in the army well it doesn't seem so very long ago since I used to play with Barbara at the bungalow down the bottom of the garden on the lawn and fancy Win getting a bigger house, she's a lad isn't she. Well dear am just writing this letter before I tuck down into bed, you see I have a furnished bed sitting room & do all my own meals. Jack has got lodgings not too far away from me & he gets full board there, so don't have to worry about him as far as that goes. I see him

2

every evening about two hours & then he has to go to work, he is night work at present, working like a nigger at the motor works. He starts work at nine o'clock at night & finishes at 7 o'clock in the morning, of course I am still working so that it only leaves us the little while in the evenings & week-ends. You say Mary in your letter why don't I get married? but how can I if my divorce hasn't gone through, do you know if it has if so perhaps you will write & let me know. Jack keeps on at me about it, you see he has about £2 a week stopped out of his money tax a week, whereas if we were married, he wouldn't. He keeps saying Phone up the solicitor that Tom had, but I won't because

3

I think if they found out where he was, they would come after him for the £400 + Jack says he wouldn't pay he would sooner serve time + I don't want him to do that especially now the baby is coming. That's another thing about getting married he said that if we were married & they took him away to serve a sentence I could claim subsistence for me + the baby but I can't do anything or claim a bean as we are now. Fancy poor old Margaret having to give up her dancing honestly when I read your letter I wished I had & chanced it + brought her away with us. All the children here have very good schools + there education is a very high standard. Don't forget not to let Tom know you have heard or he might tell the solicitor then they would know

That letter really upset me - and still does. I decided it wasn't the time to investigate more, I would leave it to rest a bit longer.

The beach hut we bought was great. It was quite basic, sort of in between, camping and a caravan. We had no running water - we used to fill up big water containers - no plumbing. There were public toilets near by, but which were a pain so we bought a 'port-a-loo,' which was good for Mel with her toilet training. After a few years, John put in a soak-away drain, much better than throwing waste into the sea at night.

We were on a private owners site at Hipkin's Beach, Walton, the huts were not rented out, so it became a little community with the owners. We only saw each other every year for six weeks, which again was very nice. The men used to swim together, the ladies used to have fun in the water with a big rubber ring, because like me, most of us couldn't swim. The children would swim together and play on the beach or around the huts, which they used to get a telling off for.

Mel's birthday was in August, so we did a party on the beach if the weather was good. Then at the end of the season, August bank holiday weekend, we would have a big bonfire and barbecue. The children were sent round the huts to collect any wood they had, the hut owners were given potatoes to jacket, we bought a big sack of potatoes, as it was cheaper that way, we also had a good deal with the local butcher, for sausages and burgers. Everybody brought their own drinks, friends of ours brought their own home-made wine, it was very good, but lethal. You made sure it was no were near the barbecue!

Helena and I did the cooking, John and Bill looked after the fire and took the food around. No music, only our wonderful sing-a-longs, and that was only after a drink or two, or more! They were really great times. Life moves on though, doesn't it.

Mel, with friends at Flamstead End Junior School, Cheshunt

Mel was coming up to the age of primary school, so we decided it was time to think about moving on to somewhere in the country, a little bit bigger too. So we chose a semi-detached in Hertfordshire, on a hill, with a little school at the bottom of the hill. At the back of us was a park where we could walk the dogs. Yes, we now had Bobby plus Trudie, yet another mongrel that John had brought home from a friend. She was lovely, but a little devil, she was always trying to get out. One day she succeeded, over the coal bunker, then over the fence. We didn't even realise she had gone until there she was, waiting at the gate, whining to come back in. We had know idea how long she had been out for, but she must have had a whale of a time - she slept for the rest of the day.

A few months later I said to John, "Trudie's getting very fat, and I'm not feeding her any more than usual food. We are due to go to the hut for six weeks so we had better get her checked out at the vet." Which he did. It wasn't a particular shock when he said she was pregnant. But it was a shock when he said, they were due any day now! John told him we were away for the next six weeks, and the vet said, "Does she know the place you are going to?" "Yes" he said. "Is it local?" "Yes," he said. "Then don't worry about it."

Trudie

Off we went in a fully loaded car. One child, two dogs, (one pregnant), and enough food and luggage for six weeks. Two days after arriving Trudie started her labour. We cleared a space, laid layers of newspapers down, then after each pup was born, we took a layer of paper off. She had trouble with one of the pups as it was breach. John said to me, "Go up to Aunt's (Florrie, who lived just above the beach hut site) and ring the vet. This one's going to need some help." I ran up the steps and across the road to Aunt's house. I ran in and explained the situation and she rang the vet immediately. The vet told me what to do. All I had to do was remember what he had told me. I was saying it all to myself all the way back to the hut. I needn't have bothered, John had already turned it around. By the time we went to bed Trudie was still very restless, we waited until she had settled down before we went to sleep.

When we woke in the morning, Mel said "We have another

and its a golden colour. Can we keep it? You promised!" Which we did. We had said to Mel that if a pup was born on her birthday - which was today - and it was a gold colour, then we would keep it. We thought she was having us on, but no, there it was, this lovely little gold puppy. It was meant to be. "OK. Happy Birthday, darling, what are you going to call him?" - we had checked to see what sex it was - "Goldie," she said, with a big grin. No surprise there then! Later that day we had to take them all to the vet to be checked over. When he checked Trudie over he said there was another pup still in her womb, but it wasn't alive. It had to be removed.

We couldn't believe it, that little one made it fourteen pups. The vet said he thought she must have conceived from more than one dog, hence the golden one. We managed to get though our six weeks holiday, packing up to come home was an adventure. One child, two adult dogs. And thirteen puppies. All loaded in the back of our Ford Cortina estate. All the rest of the pups grew nicely, and were found good homes, two of them with beach hut owners.

Puppies: Sheba, Max & Goldie - with Trudie curled up next to him.
There were fourteen pups in all.

Chapter Nine

My late thirties and early forties were taken up with the theatre. John and I had been involved with the Scout pantomime since we were married, John backstage, and me doing the cast make up. I started with the chorus make-up, then when the main man retired, I took over doing the whole cast. I really enjoyed that; making false beards, moustaches, and hair pieces, and some wonderful characters, for every panto you can name, all amateur. Although - name dropping now - I did meet Frankie Howerd, as he was taking over my dressing room as I was coming out. He called me *'Madam'*. I don't know how he meant that, but apparently he called every one madam! Say no more. The other person I met was Shirley Ann Field. She was playing principal boy and she had the shortest legs I have ever seen on a principal boy, but she was very good. The reason for the 'pros' being there was that their professional pantomime followed our own amateur effort. We did all our pantomimes at the Intimate Theatre in Palmers Green, North London. We did a two week run, very hard work.

I have lots of good memories of the panto days. There are two that stand out in my mind. A panto that's not well known was called 'Tom Thumb'. I played a comic fairy, 'Fairy Sunshine', she was such a fun character; always tripping over things, all her magic going wrong. There was one scene, where the chorus had just started to sing their song... Oh, I thought I've just got time to go to the loo. So I dashed downstairs and into the dressing room. I had just finished, when I heard the last verse of the song. I just about made it into the wings, heard my cue and on I went, doing a stage trip as I went. The chorus parted in the middle, and as I turned around with my backside facing the audience some one grabbed me from behind.

"What's going on?" I said, in a stage whisper.

"Don't worry!" Shouted the chorus.

It wasn't until after we all came off stage that they told me that my dress - which was all made of net - had got caught in my knickers! We all roared with laughter. Well, I was supposed to be a comic fairy.

Me, as Fairy Sunshine in the Scout pantomime, Tom Thumb

The other memory was of Snow White. I was playing a dwarf, with lots of singing and dancing and fun. We were into the last week, and as I ran down to take our bows, it felt like someone had kicked me in the calf. I turned round to give whoever it was a mouthful, but there was no-one there. I then realised I had pulled my calf muscle and I couldn't walk. Along came two strapping lads, both Scouters. One took one leg and the other took the other leg, I was nearly doing the splits, we then had to negotiate the narrow stairs down to the dressing room. The boys were either side and I was squashed in the middle, they weren't complaining and neither was I! One of the boys knew the nearby Tottenham Hotspur football club osteopath, and made an appointment for me for the next day.

"Bed rest for six days." said the osteopath.

"I can't do that, I have a show to do," came my reply.

"You actresses never do as your told!" He strapped it up as tight as he could.

So I went from being a young to an old dwarf, with a walking stick and pince-nez glasses. Good character acting!

As a decrepit dwarf in Snow White & The Seven Dwarves

Me, Mel and John at the Intimate Theatre, Palmers Green

There are lots of memories of the pantomimes we did at the Intimate. But the family had moved on to amateur operatics and dramatics. The operatic company performed one big show and one small show a year. Shows like the musical *'Hans Anderson'*, which had very good music. Then there was *'Hello Dolly'*, in which I played *'Ernestina.'* A wonderful, eccentric character who came on, usually in front of the curtain, said one line, then flounced across the stage and walked off. Most nights to a standing ovation. What a thrill it was to play that part. Except for the last night. The night before, the cast had all gone for a Chinese meal. Poor, dear Ernestina, I was throwing-up every time I came off stage. Bill, my stoic leading man, said when we were sitting in the booth on stage:
"Are you not feeling well?"
"No, why?" I said.
"Because you smell of sick!" I was mortified.

"I am so sorry!"

"Don't worry," he said, "I will kiss you anyway!" I was in bed for the next week with food poisoning.

The best big show we did at Borehamwood Civic Hall, was '*Chicago,*' which was great fun, I played a character called '*Go-To-Hell Kitty.*' She came onto stage in a lurex dress, sauntered across the stage, swinging a dolly bag and chewing gum, to great applause, then disappeared off stage and stripped in the wings. I already had a corset on and I had a toy shot gun behind my back. When I walked back on stage, the musical director, who I knew very well, nearly wet himself with laughter, he forgot to cue the drum 'gunshots' for me to kill everyone in the bed. I had to cue the drummer in myself... I have to say it was very funny. The corset was very uncomfortable, I now know how the characters from costume dramas feel.

We did some good shows at a small theatre in Potters Bar, Oakmere House, it's long gone now unfortunately. A two-hundred seater, you were very close to the audience, which I loved, but most of the rest of the cast didn't. We did shows like the musical '*Pippin*', which I prompted for. Then there was '*Andy Capp,*' what a good, entertaining show that was. I helped with the production, which meant I could ask a Northern brewery if they could help us out with things; bar pumps, trays and bar towels. To our surprise they also supplied enough beer for the week long show. You can imagine what a fun week we had when the beer being drunk on the set was real.

In that show I also played a brilliant character called '*Mrs Scrimmett*' who was Andy Capp's mother-in-law. A large, loud, blue-rinsed lady, with a northern accent. Such fun!

The other really lovely part I played, was the '*Wicked Witch of the West,*' from the '*Wizard of Oz.*' As I said, we were very close to the audience at that theatres and as I came in from the side door, I was cackling really loudly, enough to make a little girl in the front row of the stalls cry. I felt awful, but she soon stopped and enjoyed the show.

It wasn't until I started writing this chapter that I realised just how busy we were, as a family, through the 1980's.

Above: Hans Anderson & Pippin
Below: As Madame Thénardier, from Les Miserables & Mrs Scrimmett, Andy Capp

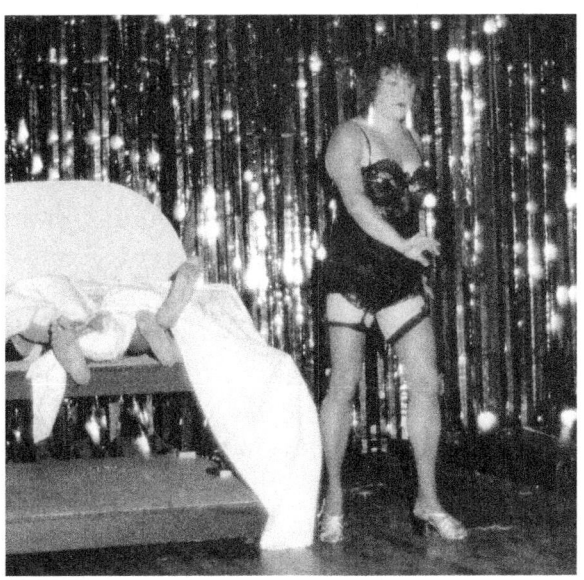

Above: As Go-To-Hell Kitty in Chicago at Borehamwood Civic Hall
Below: As The Wicked Witch of the West in the Wizard of Oz & Ernestina in Hello Dolly

I used to pop in and see Dad every few days. He was living at Nags Head Road on his own, although I did some shopping and cleaning for him. Well, this particular day when I went in, he said: "I think I have something wrong with my legs."

"Show me," I said to him, he pulled his trouser leg up and his legs were both weeping, "Right. I am taking you to the doctors, get your coat." The doctor was only just around the corner.

I got him into the surgery, I said to the receptionist, that my dad needs to see a doctor urgently, and we went straight in. He took one look at his legs and told me to take him straight to hospital, which I did.

The consultant said after he had looked at him, that he had congestive heart failure, and would not live much longer. He died on the 13th of April 1983. His ashes were put with Nanna and Grandad's.

For the operatic society I did a revue with my wonderful leading man Bill Baynes. With blacked-out teeth and straggly hair we did a duet, 'Master of the House' from 'Les Miserables,' it went down a storm with the audience, clapping and cheering - almost an encore.

I'm sure Mum would have been very proud of the characters I played and would have been pressing me to go professional. I wouldn't do it without her, so I rang the Salvation Army to see if they could help again. They said no, it would take up too much manpower to start a trace after 45 years. The Salvation Army suggested I put an advertisement in the Oxford local paper, which I did. Nothing. I made up my mind that I was not going to see her again, so we carried on living ours lives without her.

My mother-in-law was a great help and enjoyed getting involved with making costumes, mainly mine and my daughters for pantomimes, the 'Ugly Sisters' in 'Cinderella', and a tunic and blouse for Mel for '*Robin Hood*.' Mel ended up playing quite a few principal boys during in her early amateur acting career.

The end of the 1980's and beginning of the 1990's and we were all involved both on and off stage in both amateur operatic and dramatic shows. I will never forget this time in my life, but it was to completely change everything.

Me and Vivian White as the Ugly Sisters in Cinderella, another Scout pantomime

Chapter Ten

The change came when John became a driving instructor. I was also going through my exams for instructing and I passed every one except the last, which was my own test for instructing, which I failed. Not by much, but enough to make them say I had to redo them *all* again. That was that. No way. I must admit I didn't really enjoy doing the job. I got sick to death with van drivers being right up my backside when I was with a learner. It was hard work trying to put them at ease. OK, I would find something else to do.

That came in the form of millinery with a young lad of nineteen years of age who used to help us backstage at the theatre at Potters Bar. Greg and I became friends. We spent a lot of time talking, about all sorts of things, but mainly about theatre. We used to sit in his mum's conservatory and make hats, and just chat. One day we were doing just that, chatting and millinery work, Greg's mum was doing some ironing, and I thought she had the radio on.

"That radio sounds terrible!" I said to Greg.

" That's not the radio. That's my mother singing."

"Oh I'm sorry," I said, feeling embarrassed.

"Charming," Pat, his mum, said, but with a smile on her face. Even now she sounds like a broken radio when she sings, bless her!

Greg said he would like to run a theatre business, and I said so would I. And so it began. We both put some money into buying stock; costumes, hats, which were old and we would do up, shoes, gloves. We used to go to a lady in Hertford who had a pitch at a car boot sale in a school car park. She sold some lovely clothes, all washed and ironed, but mainly modern. When we started to talk to her, and we told her what business we were in, she said she had lots of vintage clothing and would we like to come and see it. "Yes please," we said, we made an appointment for the following weekend.

Mrs 'M' lived in a big Victorian house, it was absolutely crammed with clothing, mainly from the 1930's and 1940's, hats, shoes, gloves - a lot of those were very small - ladies had very small hands then. We were very excited and stunned by what she had, we just wanted to buy it all, but we had to be careful, money was tight. We went back time and again when we were looking for something special, and we knew we could get it from her. We found out as we got to know her better, that she was a retired magistrate and the Superintendent Registrar for Hertfordshire, would you believe it? She was a lovely lady and never charged us the true value of what we bought from her.

By this time, Mel was married and had a place of her own, so her room was used as a store room. We also collected stage props and small furniture until it came to the point where we couldn't get through the door for all of the stuff. So we moved everything into a lock-up unit a few miles away. It was long and narrow and smelt of damp dogs. They used to keep greyhounds in it! But it was cheap. We cleaned it up as best we could, but it was still very cold and damp and we knew we couldn't stay there very long. We started hiring out to companies we knew in the business and that Greg worked with at the theatre; he was now working as a theatre technician at Potter Bar. Once again we got too big for the lock-up, and it was too cold for the costumes and furniture, they were starting to go mouldy and were costing us money to dry-clean all the time.

Our retail outlet, in an arcade in High Street, Cheshunt

We took a lease on a small shop in an arcade, which we made to look really nice, with mannequins dressed in Victorian costume, sitting at a table in the window. We had to advertise a lot, so people would know where we were, as our shop was not on the roadside. It was a hard struggle to start with, Greg was doing two jobs: making costumes all day and working as a technician in the theatre most nights. I was also working in the café - which was also in the arcade, just along from our shop - from 7.00am until I opened the shop at 10.00am and then I worked until 5.00pm.

Anything that had to be washed or repaired I would take home. I remember taking home some feather boas to wash, I had put them on the radiator to dry before I left for work. When I got home in the evening, I walked in the front door and there were feathers everywhere! Our springer spaniel, Lucy, had ripped them all to pieces. I think Greg had been at the shop that day, and she'd got bored. She came out to greet us with her tail between her legs, and feathers stuck to her nose, she looked so funny we couldn't be cross with her, we just roared with laughter.

Greg and I were travelling the country on buying trips, looking for costumes mainly. Greg was losing interest in the props side, because we could never compete with the big companies, so we concentrated on the costumes and accessories. We used to come back with car-loads of stuff, some needing a lot of work to be done to them to make them useful, washing and ironing them and alterations, which Greg did, it was great fun. We saw lots of places, and lots of people, most of them very camp or very eccentric. We bought some of Danny la Rue's pantomime dame costumes which were one of our best buys as they were hired out a lot. We also bought the pink jacket which John Inman wore as a ballet dancer, with tights, in one of the Christmas special episodes of the BBC show '*Are You Being Served*'. The BBC used to regularly sell off the costumes that it had made for all manner of programmes, and if you knew who to talk to you could get some bargains, as the costumes had only ever been worn for one or two days.

Then it was on to Blackpool to look at some showgirl headdresses, which were nice, but far too expensive. On to Liverpool. We had heard of a company that were importing 'superhero' costumes from America, so we went to investigate. We thought they were cheap and tacky, but we might try them out in the shop. People didn't want to buy them, (in the USA, everyone buys their costumes, they never hire them), they wanted to hire them, but the quality wasn't good enough for that, all the time it was trial and error.

The last trip we made was to Alfreton in Derbyshire, to a shop full of theatre costumes and fancy dress. Why is it these people were very eccentric? This lady owner was. She wore a blue velvet turban, but had no teeth. But boy, did she have some stuff in that shop. Once again we had to think about our budget, but as usual we came back with a lot more than we bargained for. We had a job to get it all in the car, it was floor to roof inside, plus a male mannequin, (very hard to find back then) which was looking out of the side window. Then, on the roof was a 3ft by 5ft theatre 'skip', a woven wicker basket used to transport theatre costumes, 4ft deep, strapped - as we thought - tightly on the roof, but on the way back we had to keep stopping to adjust it, because it kept sliding sideways! It took us twice as long to get home, about six hours, it should only have taken three.

While all this was going on, Greg and I were growing closer together, whilst John and I where growing further apart. So in the end it was decided that it was best all round if we split up. John moved out and Greg moved in. After a while, John and I divorced, and in 1999, Greg and I got married.

Greg and I got married on 16th April 1999, and I became Margaret Lashmar

We carried on with the business, but by this time we had the shop, a retail outlet. We hired out costumes for fancy dress, theatre, parties, promotions, advertising and to schools. We also sold costumes which Greg made. In fact, one day he said "Would you mind if I made the costumes. I don't really like working in the shop." The shop was very seasonal anyway, so in the summer, I would work in the little café in the arcade, then open the shop, from 10.00am until 5.00pm, a long day.

Greg was making costumes all day, then in the evening he would work at the theatre, as a stage technician, installing sets, rigging and operating sound and lighting equipment. Then some Sundays, we would be off to some fête or another doing face painting. We were also doing theatre make-up for some of the groups we knew in the evenings.

History repeated itself when the shop became too small. The shop next door was up for lease, so we asked the owner if we could extend. It was just a matter of taking down the partition wall, which was fine, but we realised we needed extra changing rooms, and toilets and it turned out to be quite a big job, but very good when it was done. It still meant I had to get on a step ladder to get costumes from the top rails, which were men's heavy suits, we never did get that sorted!

Photo, previous page: We doubled our space when we expanded into the adjacent shop

In the winter, when the shop was busy, I had a dear friend who would come and help me. Doreen was so good in the shop and she was also a very good actress. Greg had met her at the theatre when she came to perform with a music hall troupe, the *Lissenden Players*.

My dear friend Doreen Merry and me in the shop, among the costumes

We had to fit a group of people up in 1940's clothes for a themed wedding. This one particular lady, was absolutely perfect for the role, slim and tall. Doreen said to me "Can I dress this lady?" "Of course you can" I said. Well I have to say she looked absolutely stunning, from the bar shoes, to the belted dress, and the fox fur - which she was reluctant to wear, but Doreen said the outfit wouldn't look right without it - even down to the felt hat and lace gloves. Doreen had done a really good job, she was so proud of herself. Every time we had to costume a themed wedding it was usually Doreen who would take charge.

The one thing Doreen didn't like was any one who came into the shop with a cold, coughing or sneezing. She said to me one day:

"Do you mind if I bring something in tomorrow to stop us getting these colds?"

"Of course not" I said, sneezing for the fourth time.

So the next day, in she comes, I didn't see what she had, but the next person who came in with a cold, she dashed outside and as soon as they had gone, she sprayed all around with some lovely smelling stuff.

"What's that?" I asked.

"It's a mixture of tea tree and geranium oil with water, it kills the germs." And it certainly did.

We went though the rest of the winter without colds. We couldn't help laughing, when we were waiting for the person to leave the shop so she could spray around, even if there were other people in the shop. You would see this little person pop up from behind the counter, and give a little spray and bob down again, every one would ask what the lovely smell was, and we used to say it was a room freshener, from under the counter, then she would pop up again and every one would laugh.

We had great fun in the shop, but it was very hard work. Millennium New Year was particularly hard. Nearly every costume in the shop was hired out, or sold. We had no washing machines at the shop, so everything had to be brought home and washed and dried for the next day. The back half of the house was floor to ceiling with costumes to be washed, and that's what we did the whole weekend. Doreen did help with the ironing.

After six years at the shop, the lease was up. We had a big decision to make, whether to stay for another six years or move on. And so, with a heavy heart and a big thank you, I said goodbye to my beloved friend Doreen and moved on.

Chapter Eleven

After the 2000 New Year celebrations, we were very tired, and had a big decision to make by April. I think we both wanted to move, we wanted somewhere where we could live and work. Greg made some appointments to see houses in various counties around the south of the country. On the following Sunday we travelled over 300 miles, starting just over the border in South Wales, through middle England and back with no success. Either they were too small, or too expensive. We never considered north of the border, Scotland. We probably could have got something up there, but I think we would have found it too cold. The decision had been made, we were going to move, but where to?

We starting to sell off the shop stock as we had decided not to continue the costume hire business. The fabrics, sewing machines, and haberdashery were all coming with us, because that's what we wanted to do: make costumes to sell, not run another shop. We had quite a lot of contacts already, which we knew would buy from us, all we had to do was find somewhere to go to live and work.

During the February of that year, we had to go to Walton-on-the-Naze, to Auntie Win's funeral. While we were making the journey to Walton, Greg asked me 'had we thought of Walton to live? I said no, I hadn't and that we could have a look at the estate agents while we're there, which we did. We were looking in one window and I spotted a house I knew. It was a large, semi-detached, three storey, Victorian house; we could work in the attic, then in the evening we could close the doors and we would have a nice living space with three bedrooms, and downstairs, a sitting room, dining room, breakfast room, kitchen, utility, and a lovely big garden. It was ideal, on paper. We booked an appointment for that evening after the funeral, so at 6.00pm we said our goodbyes and left to look at the house. When we went inside, it was very drab and dismal and very dark. We said we would think about it. When we came out, we looked at each other.

"I didn't like it, did you?"

"No I didn't," Greg said. "It's such a shame, as it's ideal for what we wanted." We talked about it all the way home.

"We did choose a miserable day, and it was getting dark. Maybe we should go back at the weekend and have another look."

We went back on the following Sunday. Oh my, what a difference. It was light and bright, the owners were sitting in the garden, talking to the neighbours, who by chance I knew - the lady of the house had worked with John's mum in Wood Green - so we said if the transaction is straight forward, then it is meant to be. We went ahead and made an offer which was accepted.

Back at the shop, it was business as usual, we were doing quite well at selling off the shop stock. In fact there were quite a lot of the shops closing in the arcade, the café had already gone, so I would not have a job come the summer, yet another reason for moving. We had had some vandalism too, which made me feel a little nervous as we were at in the back, so all in all it was the right thing to do.

Greg had been working with me all day, packing up stock, at about 4.00pm he said:

"I'll go home now, and see to the dog and make some food for us."

" OK, that will be good. I will finish up here, lock up and follow you." I said. About 15 minutes later the phone rang, it was Greg.

"I have just been listening to a programme on the car radio, and they have mentioned a website you can look at if you want to find someone. I have just looked at it and I think I have found your Mum and Jack. I have a telephone number, do you want me to give it to you or ring it?" My heart was pounding.

"I'm locking up and coming home!" All the while thinking it's another mistake. After all this while, how can it be?

When I got home, there it was on the screen. Sylvia Dorothy Bessie Davis and Jack Havelock Davis, and an address in Oxford. Such distinctive names, so unlikely to be a coincidence. Somehow the family knew she'd maybe gone back to Oxford to live.

"I can't ring the number. She may not want to talk to me. I'll ring cousin Pam she'll know what to do." Pam was as shocked as I was.

"I can't do it either, but I know someone who will." She was talking about her daughter, Angela, "I'll speak to her now." A few minutes later, Angie was on the phone.

"You'll have to give me time to put it to her, if it is her. I don't want her to have a heart attack with the shock of it!"

What would I say to her, after all these years? I was beginning to hope she didn't want to speak to me, at least I would know she was alive, but I didn't want to be rejected again. As these thoughts were going through my head, the phone made me jump.

I picked it up, it was Angie.

"I have just spoken to your mum, and she wants you to ring her."

"How did you manage it?" I asked her, wondering what she had said to her.

"I told her I was doing a family tree, then I asked her the names of her sisters, she said them all straight away and then she said 'if you're doing a family tree, do you know my daughter Margaret?' Yes I said, I know Margaret very well. 'Will you ask her to ring me?' I said I would."

"Thank you, Angie, I will let you know how we get on." I replied incredulously, and put the phone down.

I went and made a cup of tea, then with hands shaking, I picked up the phone and rang the number, it rang for a while, then a voice said 'Hello.' Somehow I knew it was Mum's voice - it sounded just like Auntie Mary.

"Hello, Mum?" I sounded just like a little girl again.

"Oh! Is that you Margaret, it's lovely to hear from you."

From then on, it was as if I had only spoken to her the day before. After that we spoke on the phone nearly every day. Of course we had fifty years of catching up to do.

The next thing we had to do was make an arrangement with Mum to meet me and her last remaining sister Flo, but before that she had to tell her family. She had four sons with Jack, all married with children. She said the family were going to have a big party for her upcoming 80th birthday and she was going to tell them all about me.

On the 12th March it was Mum's 80th Birthday and the family had arranged a meal at the local hotel. Later Mum recalled:

"We were all sitting round the table, when I said to Sue (her daughter in law), 'I've been speaking to my daughter today' she looked at me as if I were mad."

"You haven't got a daughter, Mum," Sue replied, assuming senility had kicked in.

"Yes, I have, and I spoke to her and we are going to meet up soon."

Well! You can imagine all the questions from the family, and when I spoke to Sue some time later, she said she had thought there was some sort of secret, between Mum and Jack. But she thought it was that perhaps Mum and Jack weren't married. It had never occurred to them all that it was something like this.

The first meeting we had with Mum, was at Angie's, who by chance, happened to live just a few miles away from Mum in Oxfordshire. The meeting was with Auntie Florrie, my cousins Pam and Sue, and Angie's daughter Laura, all the closest family she had.

Left to right: Pam, Laura, Auntie Florrie, Mum, Me, Sue, Angie

Greg and I were the last to arrive because of heavy traffic. When we got there, Mum was coming down the stairs, she took one look at me and said "And who are you?" "Margaret," I said, and she nearly fell down the stairs. There were lots of hugs and kisses and tears, not just from me and her, but from all the family. We looked at heaps of photos, told lots of stories, a whole life-time in one afternoon.

The rest of April 2000 was a round of meetings. Mum went to stay with Auntie Florrie, and there they met lots more of the family, there are so many of them. Later in April we went to Oxford to meet Mum's eldest son, my half-brother, Jack. We were a bit nervous, because we realised he had no idea of the story. Mum had not told another living soul anything about her family or marriage to my Dad, or me for the last fifty years.

So we took all the photos and papers we had. I felt I had to prove I was her daughter. The meeting went well and we all went out to lunch. I think he could see how natural we were together. We found out that Mum had only been put on the 'phone a week before she received Angie's call. This was all meant to be, to me it was fate.

My half-brother Jack and his wife, Sue

There was no-one left in my Dads family to object to me finding mum. All the aunts and grandparents were dead including Dad, so I felt I could go ahead without feeling guilty.

During May and June of that year, we were involved in a fashion show for the British Costume Association, producing a catwalk show, finding models and rehearsing them, making costumes for them and the show. For me, it was writing the script, making my own costume, a lot of work for both of us, plus Greg was still working. We had sold our house and were packing up our contents. Looking back, I don't know how we did it, but as always, we did, and enjoyed it. During this time I spoke to Mum on the 'phone and I managed to get a letter to her, explaining to her that we wouldn't be able to see her until after we moved, which we hoped would be the 17th of July.

We did move in on the 17th as planned, None of the family living at Walton-on-the-Naze knew, we wanted it to be a surprise. The very next day we invited everybody round, they were a bit shocked that we were inviting them to a totally random address, but they came anyway. When we told them that this lovely house was ours now, it was all hugs and kisses, they were all so pleased we were now living down here, all together.

On the 28th of July, Mum came down by train and saw the house and we all had a family lunch at the pub. Mum came back with us and we walked our dog Lucy on the Naze then in the evening we went across onto the green to watch the fireworks at the end of the pier. This was a ritual every Sunday summer evening, it was usually a wonderful display, but only lasted about fifteen minutes, but still well worth watching.

Mum was staying with Auntie Florrie for the night as we had no spare beds yet. When we picked her up the next day, I managed to talk to Auntie Florrie about Mum.

"This morning she was sitting on the side of my bed and I wanted to give her a big hug, but I couldn't. I felt she wasn't my Sylvie any more," Florrie said to me.

"That's how I feel. I feel she's not my mother. Do you think that will go away?"

"I'm sure it will, just give it time." We ran Mum to the station, she had a horrible journey home, there are no direct trains to Oxfrod from Walton, and she didn't come by train again.

We had had a really nice few days, it was very relaxed and we felt comfortable with each other, you would never have thought we had not seen each other for fifty years.

Mum was due to come and see me on the 14th of October,

but had to cry off because Jack wasn't well. He had been drinking and not eating and was a bit hurtful with her. What that meant I'm not sure. Poor Mum she had a lot to put up with him.

We were due to see her on the 31st of October, but they had had terrible storms in Oxford, and it was impossible for us to see each other. All the news came via 'phone and letters, it seemed every time we arranged to meet something happened. In November she had shingles, a nasty illness, so we knew we weren't going to see her before Christmas.

We had a good time around a roaring log fire in our new home. We did miss her not being with us. Maybe next year.

Chapter Twelve

The year 2001 was a very difficult year for us. We had lots of work going on in the house, both inside and out, we were also trying to earn a living. Greg was going up to the theatre to work, which was about nearly two hours away but it was only for a week. He was not at all settled. We were still making up costumes for customer orders and for the BCA show in the spring at the Malvern showground. We also needed to get the new catalogues produced and sent out with our new range of costumes in. A lot of work to be done, and quickly. We couldn't be without money for too long.

I kept in touch with Mum by 'phone or letter, and it was very difficult for her to come to us because she couldn't leave Jack for long because of his not eating and drinking too much, it would send him into a depression. Mum was used to it. Apparently he had been like it for a long time. Her salvation was the church. She helped a lot with making tea for all sorts of classes and groups, arranging flowers for the services. Being able to talk to the other people who worked there, it gave her a social life. She also loved her keep-fit and line dancing, and she did that well into her nineties and loved it. She even did a couple of courses at the local university! One was German, which she never ever spoke, not to me anyway, and the other was 'Jazz Appreciation' or something similar. As far as I know she liked jazz, but she just did it for something to do and people to meet, she also got a hot meal, which saved her from cooking. She said it was good, on one of them she even got a bed for the night as it was a weekend course. She lived her life to the full.

She had to. Life with Jack was not good. On the day of her birthday in March, she went to lunch with her daughters-in-law, Gee and Lyn, and she said she came home to Jack saying he wasn't well, and with that he went to bed with a bottle of whisky, Mum went to bed with a book.

In May of that year I was talking to Mum on the 'phone. Suddenly she said:

"Just a minute Mags, Jack wants to talk to you," Jack came to the phone.

"I'm so sorry Margaret for what I have done to your life, don't blame your Mum. She's a good woman."

"I know. I don't blame her. What's happened has happened, you can't turn back the clock," I replied, astonished.

"Thank you for saying that." Jack said, then he put Mum back on the 'phone.

"That was nice of him, wasn't it?" I bit my tongue...

"Yes," I said, and we said no more about it.

In the September of that year, Jack died of a blood clot to the brain. It seemed strange that he should say those things to me, it almost seemed as if he knew he was going to die. I will never forgive him, he ruined all of our lives. I know it takes two, but I sort of think she didn't have much choice but to leave with him, she was pregnant with his child.

I didn't know my half-brothers that well then. Mum said

they didn't want me to go to the funeral and she was quite upset about it. I told her not to be upset, I wouldn't go anyway, he wasn't my Dad, my Dad passed away back in the 1980's.

Mum was a much more free person once Jack went. We saw more of her, we went places with the family, and she was able to see more of her remaining sister Flo, although she was in her nineties and in not such good health, but we did have good times.

Pam and Sue decided to get the doctor in to Auntie Florrie as she seemed to be in quite a lot of pain. He told them she had a blockage in her bowel and would need an operation, but he said it was not a good idea because of her age, Aunt said she didn't want one anyway. So it was decided that between the three of us, we would look after her. I did a lot of her meals. She loved her three-minute egg for breakfast, she didn't mind what she had for lunch as long as she had something sweet for afters - usually an egg custard - which slipped down easily, or a light steamed pudding and custard. As time went on and she took to her bed, she'd eat egg custards most of the time. It was really hard for all of us to see her losing her will to live.

One day, I remember taking her in a home-made fish cake and some creamy mash potatoes.

"How was that? Did you like it?" I asked her.

"No." She said. "What's for pudding?"

"Ice cream," I said. She ate it with gusto. "How was that?" I asked again.

"Lovely!" she said. All the sisters loved their ice cream.

All through that year it was work, work and work. We were sending costumes to Europe, America, all the British counties, plus extra orders at Hallowe'en and Christmas. We didn't have a lot of spare time. We did do some rowing on the Walton Backwaters in the summer and Greg still had the allotment which was very time consuming, but fun when we the plot holders used to have their annual get-together with music and dancing. I spent as much time as I could in the garden, which I loved. We did managed to get to one or two garden and craft fairs, but always the day after we had to catch up on work.

Rowing on the Walton Backwaters with Pam and her husband Roy, I'm coxswain!

Auntie Florrie was fading fast, on morphine now, sleeping most of the time, not eating, and just a few sips of water, it was very depressing to watch. On one of her good days, she managed to speak to Mum on the phone, just a few words, more or less to say goodbye. Auntie Florrie, dear Auntie Florrie. More than a mum to me than my own mum, passed away peacefully in her sleep. She knew when the end was coming because she had sent us all away except Sue and Mandy, who she knew could cope, even on her death bed she was a very shrewd lady.

Mum was coming down for Auntie Florrie's funeral, but first we are going to cheer her up a bit by taking her to see Mel in her show, at our old theatre. The show was 'Half a Sixpence' and she was playing the lead role, 'Ann.' I wanted to see it as it's one of my favourite shows, and I thought we all needed cheering up.

Aunt was laid to rest on the 13th of November, near to her grandson, Edward which she wanted. Mum got very upset, she cried and cried on my shoulder, and at one point Greg had to physically hold her up. She knew that she was the last sister, and how she had missed so many years with them.

There were lots of family there of course, and some who didn't know Mum was there, so we had lots of questions, which at this time she didn't want to answer. We said we would have a get together, and they would all be invited.

Mum went home with cousin Angie on the train, we drove them to the station, she would be back with us at Christmas.

The next day, I sat and wrote a poem, remembering Aunt. Whenever we went to visit her, she would always have a dew drop on her nose - its a family trait - so this is the poem...

Hello Margaret. Come in, come in!
Just a minute, while I wipe my nose before I kiss you.
Sit down and tell me all your news.
I was so happy to hear about this.
And so very sad about that.
Always so interested,
Always full of fun.

Never about herself,
But everyone.
Thank you Auntie Florrie for your good advice and points of view.
Just a minute while I wipe my nose
Before I kiss you.

Down to earth and back to work. Walton in Bloom panto costumes to make plus the usual Christmas costumes. Puddings and cakes to make for us. Lots of places to go and people to see, busy, busy, busy.

Throughout the end of the year we were inundated with orders for 'Elvis' costumes. Greg wasn't that keen, but I enjoyed doing them, as there was a lot of hand sewing, some of the designs were amazing, even if I do say so myself! Would you believe we were sending them to America? Bonkers eh! We weren't complaining, they were expensive! Mum did come for Christmas, she said it was the best Christmas she'd ever had. It made me cry.

Chapter Thirteen

In my early years, families would not move very far away from one another, one because they didn't have cars, and two because you were always on hand when needed. Like I was, when my cousin needed me to help with the children or when my grandad needed me to look after Nan, so he could go to the pub for a pint and a natter with his mates. It was important to be close to your family.

Nowadays it is a struggle to get to family when they need us. We live in rural Essex, my daughter lives in Hertfordshire, which is only an hour and a half away, but too far to pick my grandson up from school or pop round for a bit of child minding. We see him once a month, and then he doesn't want to go home, but thats how it is, we all have a living to earn.

Greg is in an even worse position. His mum and sister, niece and nephew live in Yorkshire and County Durham, so he sees them twice a year if he's lucky. It's a six hour journey, which we all hate. My mum and half-brothers live in Oxford, which is a three hour trip by car on a good day. But we all made our choices to where we wanted to live so we have to put up with it.

The one consolation is that we have telephone, text, email

or good old fashioned letters, and if needs be, cars. Thank goodness for friends you can call on in times of trouble.

2003/4 were years when we were doing all sorts of jobs to make ends meet. Our main job was costumes, which I enjoyed, but Greg was loosing interest and he was working at the local theatre, in place of the manager, who was unwell and on long term sick leave. I think he liked it because he was getting a more regular income and I did understand, but I was sorry about the costumes. We were getting orders for a good range of costumes, more expensive costumes, but needs must when the devil drives.

We spent a lot of time with the family, it was tea every Wednesday, and one of the family would do a meal once a month. If Mum was with us, she would come along too, she had a whale of a time.

In the spring we thought about letting our springer spaniel Lucy, have a litter of puppies. She was six years old and it was her last year, she would have to be spayed next year, so we looked into it. There was a sire near by, with a good pedigree, so we gave it a try. She wasn't overly impressed! We said, lets see what happens if it doesn't work, then we won't do it again. We were encouraged when the vet said there maybe one or two puppies in there. We were looking forward to it. But on the second visit, we were told that she wasn't pregnant, we were disappointed, but we kept to our word and didn't try again. I'm very glad we didn't, as some time after she was very unwell, and had a nasty infection in her womb. She had to have an emergency operation to remove the womb and ovaries. She was fine for about a year, then she began to do all kinds of strange things, like picking up bits of her dinner, dropping it on the floor, under the furniture, something she had never done before. Back to the vet for more tests, the results came back, they thought she'd had a stroke, and they wanted to keep her in for a while longer. She was at the vets for three or four days, we kept ringing, they kept telling us that she was comfortable. In the end we just had to see her, and when we did, we couldn't believe what we saw. Poor Lucy didn't know who we were, all she wanted to do was to go back to the kennel with the nurse.

"What is wrong with her? What have you done to her?" we asked, desperately.

"Nothing," the vet said, "We think she has had another stroke."

"Will she get any better?" We had to ask.

"No, we don't think so." It was then we made the decision to have her put to sleep and stop her suffering any more. We were left wondering 'why didn't they tell us sooner?' Money. I think the longer they keep her in the hospital, the more it costs. We should have sued them, but you are so upset, you don't think about it do you?

In 2005 we changed direction again. We also started keeping hens, just two to start with, Barbara and Margo, named after *The Good Life* characters. Babs was a Wellsummer and Margot a Light Sussex, they were lovely birds, and good layers. Greg made them a nice little house, one you could move around, which kept the grass down. We had to stop Lucy from chasing them - one day she had Margo pinned to the floor - but after a good telling off she never ever did it again, and they got on fine. Jake our other springer spaniel dog wouldn't go anywhere near them in fact, he was afraid of them, which we didn't mind, it saved a lot of hassle having to train him not to chase them.

With fresh eggs in the morning, and the rooms ready, one double with private bathroom, and one king, we started doing bed and breakfast. We had a lot of nice people stay, and also some not so nice ones. A couple booked in for one night, and when they turned up he was carrying a guitar on his shoulder which he promptly started playing at midnight. It didn't go on for too long, thank goodness, and it was only for the one night. They were very noisy love-makers too, thankfully they never came back!

After a while we stopped taking one-nighters. No profit in that. There was another time we had a problem. I was hanging the washing on the line when a woman came to the gate...

"Excuse me, would you have two rooms for the end of this week? It's for myself, my husband, and daughter, for four nights. My company are paying for me to recover after an operation." I said we did and booked her in for the four nights once showing her the rooms. She arrived on the Saturday, not with her husband and daughter as expected but with a female friend! And now they only wanted one room. As you can imagine we were very suspicious, but they gave us the company cheque. When they had gone out Greg rang the company and told them that we were not happy with the situation. They said that was not what she had told them and that we must do what we think is best, and that the cheque would be honoured whatever we decided. Greg looked the company up on line, it was a good company, so we went ahead with the booking. Well, the two women came in very late and had obviously been drinking, not the sort of thing you would do when your recovering from an operation. They were talking and laughing and on their mobiles until the early hours of the morning, so not much sleep for us. The morning came and we told them that we were sorry but they couldn't stay with us any longer. Well, they started ranting and raving and demanded their money back in cash! We replied that we would take the money for the one night they stayed and they could have the rest, but only after we'd informed the company. After a lot of abuse, they left. We did check the room after they left, and nothing was damaged.

We had one couple who came year after year and would stay a week, even on their diamond wedding anniversary. We cooked them a nice evening meal and we have been good friends ever since.

We did B&B for nearly six years. Its very hard work, even though we were only small. I was coming up to sixty and thinking of retiring, and doing only what I wanted to do. Reading, writing, gardening, and looking after the chickens - we had five by then.

Both Greg and I had big birthdays that year, one at the beginning and one at the end, so we decided to celebrate them both in the middle of the year, June in fact, with an all day party, starting at ten in the morning and finishing, well, whenever!

Our combined 30th and 60th birthday party with family and friends

Some people were staying over, and we couldn't have wished for a better day weather-wise, it was a really warm sunny day. It was a day to remember, with family and friends meeting up, some for the first time, others we hadn't seen in a long time. Everyone helping with refreshments, serving drinks, some stayed just an hour or two, some, like my mother, stayed a week.

That week I think was the best time I had ever had with Mum. We went out with the family to Beth Chatto's garden, which we all love. We had a lovely time on Angie's boat, with a trip to see the seals on the Backwaters. I have a lovely picture of her pulling her hat right down over her ears, to stop the wind getting in. During that week we drank a lot of tea, and ate a lot of cake. At a great barbecue at Pams, Mum got a bit tiddly and we nearly had to carry her home, I think she'd had a good time.

On the boat, Walton Backwaters, spot the cake!

Mum spent a lot of time during that week just sitting with Jake, our second springer spaniel, and the chickens in the garden, contemplating. I really don't think she wanted to go home and we had spoken about her moving down here. I think she thought she shouldn't because of her family, and the church, and the friends she'd made, so we didn't mention it again.

At Beth Chatto's garden. Left to right: Mum, Me, Tap; Pam's mother-in-law, Pam

We were starting to wind down the costume business but I was still sewing sequins and jewels onto Elvis costumes to send to the USA. I still can't believe we did that, but the feed back we used to get was "we make them better than they do." I felt that was a great compliment.

The winter of 2006 was taken up with writing panto scripts. This year it was going to be '*Snow White and the Seven Dwarfs.*' These scripts were rewrites of old scripts which I did as a teenager, we would update both words and music and that would take from

February until spring. We earned no money from this, it was all in aid of Walton in Bloom. Our earnings came from running our B&B, and whatever work Greg was doing at the time, which was generally working for the town council at the local theatre.

We ran the B&B from Easter to October, and in the summer I made cakes for the beach café, so you can tell we had to be quite organised. In between times, if I was lucky I could spend some time in the garden, or watching my chickens – we had baby chicks then, - I remember once when they were wandering around the garden, a big bird of some sort had dropped a cream bun outside the back door, the baby chick picked it up – it was nearly as big as she was – and ran off with it, promptly followed by mummy hen. It was too big for baby to carry very far, so she dropped it. Mum picked it up and ran off with it, promptly followed by me! Mum dropped it and I picked it up and put it in the bin, "that's put a stop to your little game," I said, and the hen clucked at me. I wasn't sure whether that was a 'thank you,' or a 'you bitch, I was enjoying that game,' she let me pick her up, so I will take it as a 'thank you.'

The other habit they had was laying their eggs all over the garden in different places. We had to do a daily search to find them all, which wasn't easy as we had so many big bushes, but we knew if the guests were to have any breakfast then we must find some. Once we had found some they had to be cracked into a bowl just to be sure they were not off, you certainly knew if you had an off one, the smell was unbearable, as you can imagine both us and the guests ate quite a lot of scrambled eggs and omelettes, not with bad eggs I hasten to add!

I used to watch the birds a lot in the garden, one day I came running in and told Greg:

"We have a family of titmars in the garden."

"What are you talking about?" He asked.

"We have a family of bluetits in the nesting box, in the tree, I have called them the 'titmars' because they live here." He came to see, I think even he was pleased, all the years we had had the boxes on the trees, the birds never used them, now they had, wonderful!

As you can imagine when you are cooking a lot, you need a lot of shopping. I was getting ready to go shopping when I heard a noise from outside, I looked out of the window and a BT lorry was blocking the drive and was just about to tip a load of tarmac across the driveway. I dashed out and very politely asked them if they would move their lorry as I had to get my car out. I got into my car and waited, but they didn't see me do that. The man doing the tipping, mimicked to the driver what I had said, and laughed, and then they saw me looking at them from my car... You have never seen them move so fast, they had that lorry away in no time at all. I waved them goodbye, and it really made me laugh. They say that mimicry is the finest form of flattery - oh boy did I feel flattered now.

Mum wanted to come for a holiday for two weeks. We arranged a date and I said I wouldn't take any guests for those two weeks. Greg took two weeks holiday, so we could take her out and about, and try and talk to her about her past.

We did have a good time together, but she had blanked out a lot of her past. We gathered together with the family, with lots of photos, and stories, which she couldn't remember but enjoyed hearing about. Once or twice she seemed to remember a name and what happened, but then it was gone. I know she wasn't senile, it was all so painful to remember, we could understand that. The family all had each other, she had had no-one but her best friend. We met this lady at Mums 90th birthday celebration and it appeared that Mum had told her the whole story.

Once again she didn't want to go home. One of her sons

had arranged to pick her up at South Mimms service station which was about halfway between Walton and Oxford, and we were taking her there. On the way our brand new car broke down, and we called the RAC. I could tell Mum was getting a little stressed, wondering whether she would ever get home. We rang Joe – Mums' son – to tell him that we would be delayed so he could get a message to his driver who was taking Mum back home to Oxford.

The RAC repaired the car as best as he could, but it was a computer fault, which could only be repaired by a Nissan garage. Eventually we managed to get to South Mimms, where the car broke down again. The driver offered to stay with us, but we said we would be alright, I was more concerned that he got Mum home. As usual we both had to 'spend a penny', but the ladies were out of order, so we had to use the gents, which had no locks on the doors. So Mum kept dog-eye for me and I for her, that was horrible. We said goodbye, with a little tear, never knowing when we will see each other again. We waited a good long time until the recovery truck arrived and they brought both the car and us home. I rang Mum to say we were safely back, and she said she was worried. I knew she was, and I did wonder if she would come to Essex again.

Chapter Fourteen

Mum was 88 years of age in 2008, and for some reason she was having trouble walking. She had a motorised scooter, and a push-along trolley. Oddly, when she was on the dance-floor, her legs seemed to work perfectly!

She enjoyed line-dancing and was very good at it, once she's on the floor, she dances the whole time, nearly two hours. Then there's the tea dances, and once she's on the floor she always finds someone to dance with. She loves to dance.

Then of course, there's keep fit. She did that sitting on a chair and she used to go to yoga too, but once she sat on the floor, someone had to help her up, so she decided she had better give that up. What an amazing lady. She was always saying to me:

"Do more exercise!"

"Yes, mother," I would say. As if I didn't do enough - clearing and cleaning a three storey house, running a B&B, directing a panto every year, walking two dogs, feeding and cleaning chickens, I was glad to sit down in the evenings.

It was as we expected when she was nervous about coming to us because of what happened earlier with the car breaking down. I think she thought she was a burden, which she wasn't, I certainly understood how she felt.

Greg and I bought a camper van from a friend of ours, and after a few short trips out Greg felt confident enough to drive the three hour journey to see Mum in Oxford. We stayed on a caravan site which had a hard standing pitch, and within an hour the little awning was up and we were sitting having a well earned cup of tea. I didn't sleep very well, what with traffic noise, and the planes coming over us from nearby RAF Brize Norton.

The next morning we drove over to pick up Mum, she lived about 30 minutes away in Kennington, and took her to the nearest pub for lunch. As ever she was really pleased to see us, and it was a very nice day, so we sat in the garden for lunch, then had a lovely walk along the river Thames at Sandford Lock. We sat on a bench watching the boats go though the lock, Mum was getting a bit tired and chilly, so we took her back home for some tea. It was sheltered in her big garden, under a tree, and we chatted for ages, about her family, and her life before she retired. She had worked at the one of the university offices, and had made quite a few friends.

Once she retired, the Church seemed to take over her life. She made coffee for the clubs, did the flowers for services and weddings and generally made herself useful. They were very pleased to have her there. After a lovely day, we headed back to the site for a large gin and tonic and a barbecue.

We talked one day about how Mum seemed so content living where she was, with her family and friends, and although she missed Jack for someone to talk to, she didn't miss his behaviour. She knew she could go wherever she wanted and with whoever she wanted and not have to worry about getting back to him.

The next day, we collected Mum and took her to Shotover Park, a country park on the outskirts of Oxford, just right for a picnic, with lots of wide open spaces, you can see for miles. We were at the top of the hill and with the van close by, so Mum and I sat on a bench, while Greg made some tea. The three of us sat in the sunshine, watching the birds in the trees - it was unbelievable weather - it must have been thirty degrees. Then it was back to Mum's for hugs and kisses and to say goodbye, we always left with a tear in our eye, never knowing when would be the next time we'd see each other.

Photos on previous page: Shotover Park, Oxford

It was 2010 when that happened, the year of Mums 90th birthday and she was having a party at her church hall in Kennington, and Greg and I had been invited. Greg had had a brilliant idea for a present, just what do you buy a ninety year old? He suggested that we put together a photograph album for Mum. Sue – her daughter-in-law – had said to us that she thought it was odd that Mum didn't have any photos, but of course Sue hadn't known the reason why until I came along a few years earlier.

My strange expression is due to the fact that I'm wondering what that is in Mum's hair!

At that time we still didn't know the rest of her family very well, and we were very nervous. We had finished the album and it looked very good, full of photos including some of Mum's parents and of her as a small child.

We arranged with our friends Chris and Frances, who live in

Shenley, near Watford - which is about half-way between here and Oxford – that we would go and leave Jake, the dog, with them, go to the party, then come back stay the night with them and come home the next day. Which is what happened.

Everyone was there, and lots of friends and family where there when we walked in. Some already knew who I was and some didn't. Those who didn't were whispering in corners, and those who did were eager to come and say hello. Of course Mum was pleased to see us, and the album and said "I'll look at it later," but the family grabbed it quick and took it into the kitchen. We were offered some tea, and a friend of Mum's came and talked to us.

This was the lady who knew the whole story and understood what had happened. She said to me that Mum had said it broke her heart to leave me behind, but Jack had said she must. That it wouldn't be a life for a little girl, living in caravans and travelling about. Mum had said she hoped they would settle down and find a house in Oxford somewhere and Jack said he has to go where the work is. It was him that wouldn't let her get in touch with her family, because of the money he owed my dad. Jack had said the police would put him into jail and Mum felt guilty about that and she didn't want him put away. The lady – I can't remember her name – was very kind and said that many times Mum had cried on her shoulder, because she missed me and her sisters so very much. She couldn't believe we had met up after all these years.

This lady said that she felt she knew me from what Mum had told her and she was very pleased to meet me.

I was quite stunned to hear what she was saying, Mum had never spoken to me about what had happened when she left, only that she said "stay with Daddy."

I have to say, the family were very welcoming, and wanted to know how we had found her. They knew there was a secret between Mum and Jack but they had thought it was because Jack and Mum weren't married - they were in fact - but I think they were afraid to ask.

Happy 90th Birthday Mum

It turned out to be a great afternoon, we all had our photo taken together and with hugs and kisses all round we left to go back to our friends in Shenley. On the way back we realised how hungry we were, not having had time with all the talking to eat anything at the party. We were in luck, as my 'new' nephew Ben had made us a bag of food from the buffet, which went down a treat. Chris and Francis had a gin and tonic ready for us, and a nice casserole, which again was very welcome. After dinner we sat and relayed the story to them, they were very pleased we were made welcome, and after a very exhausting day, we had a good nights sleep. Breakfast, and a walk with the dogs - theirs and ours - we set off home.

I rang Mum when we got home and said what a good time we had had, she said she had had a good time too. I didn't tell her what her friend had said, I thought maybe, one of these days she will tell me herself, but she never really did.

Apart from local holidays, we always tried to go somewhere where we could easily visit Mum. It seemed to be the right thing to do. We always had a nice time together. She was after all in her nineties now and we never knew how long we would have her for.

Overleaf: My new, extended family. Mum had married the lodger, Jack Havelock Davis and had four sons with him.

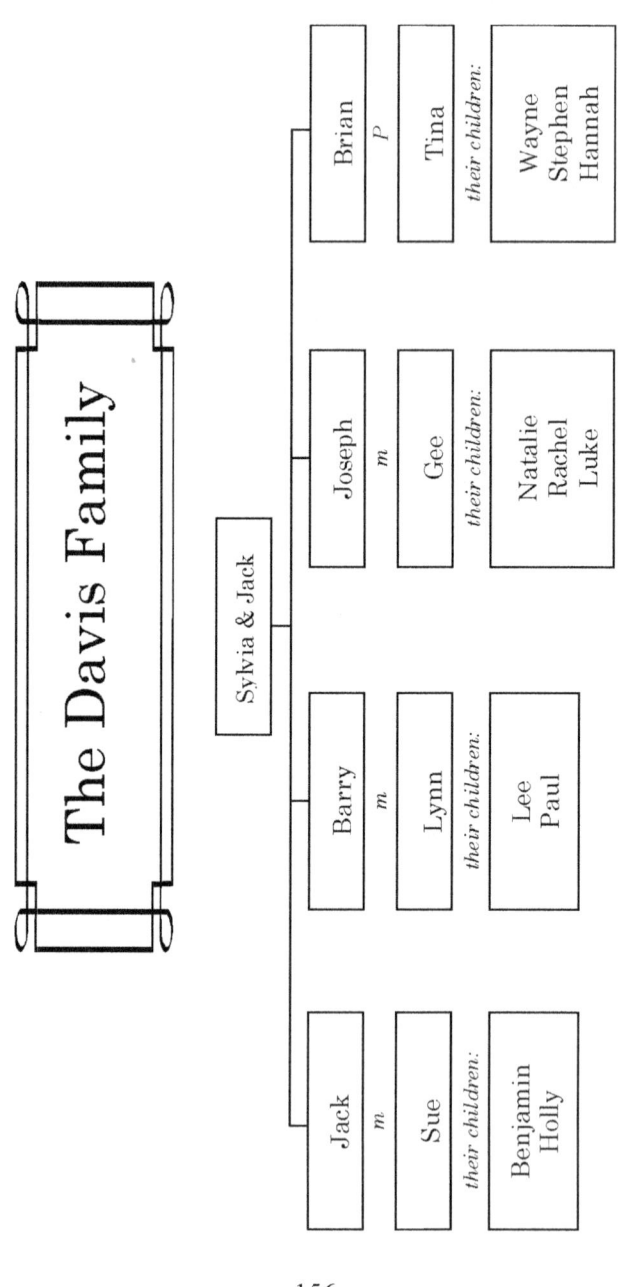

Chapter Fifteen

I have always wondered what my dad and grandparents would have said if they had met Mum after all those years. I think Dad would have asked her why she didn't come back, and told her that she could have done. There was always that love/hate relationship. He would have had her back I'm sure, that is why he never married again. He did have lady friends but no-one lasted very long. As for Nanna and Grandad, they would have told her what a lovely little girl she had had and what a life she had missed. They were very placid people, always said what will be, will be. It was very hard for Nanna, because of her arthritis she was always in such a lot of pain, but you never heard her complain. It must have been hard for them having to look after a six year old. They were good people, I will always be grateful to them.

One day when Mum and I were talking, I asked her whether she remembered Nanna Edwards. She said, "Oh yes, I remember Mrs Edwards," why didn't she call her 'mum'? Perhaps she didn't know her that well – "She was a really nice lady and a very good cook." I agreed with that.

On May 17th 2013, to be precise, we moved from our three storey, five-bedroom house, into our two-bedroomed bungalow and there was a lot of work to be done. We were going to have to live in our caravan for three or four months until the bungalow was virtually rebuilt inside. We moved in in the August, although we didn't have a kitchen, but it was so hot by then that we could eat our meals outside and cook on a patio gas griddle all day which was great.

Mum never saw the bungalow. She had gone off with Brian and Tina – her youngest son and his partner – to Kent for a weeks holiday in a caravan. I had a letter from her saying that 'it's a nice place', but she is not feeling too good and will be glad to get home.

It was now the beginning of September, and getting quite cool, so I was very glad the new kitchen was finished, and we could start living indoors for the autumn and winter.

On the 27th of October, Greg had gone to the other side of Essex to get some wood flooring for our hallway, and was driving home when he had a call on his mobile. It was Jack - Mum's eldest son - saying that Mum had had a stroke, and was in the John Radcliffe hospital, she wasn't too bad, but it had affected her speech quite severely.

We once again we made arrangements with Chris and Frances, our good friends in Shenley, to take Jasper, our cocker spaniel, to them and then go on to the hospital to see Mum. We set off and got to Frances about 11.30am, had some coffee, and then got to the hospital about 1.00pm. Visiting was at 2.00pm, so we went up to the café and had a light lunch and another drink. By the time we got down to the ward it was time to go into see her.

She gave us a big grin, in fact she looked really well, she could move her arms and legs fine, and her face looked good, but her speech had gone and she had to try and write everything down. At one point she was trying to ask us something, but we had no idea what it was she wanted. She beckoned over one of the nurses, and was trying to explain to him what she meant, but no, he didn't get it either. We got her a pen and paper, but she couldn't write it so we said 'draw it,' she drew a circle and that was it. Well! We were stumped as to what she was trying to say. Just then the lady with the tea trolley came in, and Mum got very excited, she pointed to her and then us.

"Oh!" We said "You want a cup of tea?!" she shook her head and pointed to us. "Do we want a cup of tea?" she nodded madly, "No thank you, we've just had one!" We all laughed so much it bought tears to our eyes, we realised all she wanted to do was get us a cup of tea. Bless her.

While we were there, the physiotherapist came in, "come on Mrs Davis we are taking you down the corridor, for some therapy." Well, before you could say 'tea', she was up, out of bed, grabbed her sticks and was nearly running down the corridor. I said to Greg "Well there isn't much wrong with the body." Greg was watching her go, "no, you're right, and they can work on her speech." We felt much more encouraged, that she was going to get better.

We kissed and hugged and said a long and tearful goodbye, then we were on our way back to Chris and Frances feeling much more upbeat. We eat and drunk, and talked and slept, we were very tired, it had been an exhausting day.

When we got home I rang Sue, my half-sister-in-law, and we both agreed that when Mum is better, there is no way she can go home and look after herself, she needed a care or nursing home where she could be looked after and have people around her all the time and be fed properly.

About a week later, Greg had another phone call from Jack. Shocking news. Mum had had a major heart attack, luckily while still in hospital. Jack had spoken to the consultant and been told she had about twenty four hours to live.

What do I do? Do I go, or do I stay? Eventually, after what

seemed like hours of indecision, I decided I would rather remember her as I last saw her – happy and cheerful.

Mum passed away at 6.30pm on Remembrance Sunday, the 10th November, 2013. I'm so glad we went to see her after her stroke. I think without knowing it, we had both said our 'goodbyes' then.

It was the second time we had said goodbye. The first time I was five years of age, the second time I was 68 years of age and she she was 93 years of age. We had 14 years together after we met up again. I do regret not having longer with her.

The funeral was planned for the 28th of November, and I asked Pam and some of the family if they would come and represent the family, she said she would.

So once again we had to call on our dear friends in Hertfordshire to dog-sit, and put us up for the night. On the way home we were to be picking up grandson Laurence and bringing him home for the weekend, as Mel was doing a concert. That was the plan.

Sue asked me to write a eulogy for Mum's funeral. I sat and thought about it, a lot. Nothing came into my mind at that moment. I tried and tried, but the words just didn't sound right. I keep on trying. I sat with a glass of sherry, whilst Greg cooked the dinner, and put pen to paper and the words just flowed. I was very pleased with my writing in the end, it came from the heart.

Mums funeral was the 28th November, and we met up with Pam, Angie and her partner Archie at the church, where Mum was such a stalwart. I was glad they were there, I felt that they were truly representing Mums sisters, and they were my close family, supporting me too.

After the first hymn, *'All Things Bright and Beautiful'* the order of service said 'Memories of Sylvia' and this was my eulogy:

Sixty five years ago, Mum was taking me to dancing and singing classes. Then two years later it all stopped. Mum left home. It was a sad time for her and for her family that she left behind, and of course me and Dad.

For the next 50 years we both lived our own lives, without any contact with each other, but not without thoughts and love. Then, fourteen years ago, with the help of my husband and the internet, we were reunited, along with her eldest sister and her nieces and great nieces. We were all nervous, but once we all relaxed, there were lots of hugs, kisses and stories of days gone by.

These past 14 years have been the very best, both for me and the rest of the family, knowing that Mum was back in our lives, and that we didn't have to worry about her any more, that she was safe.

What a legacy she has given me. When she left I was an only child. Now I am part of a big family and like Mum, I love them all.

Then it was to the grave to say our final goodbye. Pam and I stayed close to each other. I felt as if I was saying goodbye to my two mums, Florrie and Sylvie. I think we all felt a bit numb. Back to the church hall for a cup of tea and a chat with the family, and we vowed we would keep in touch. I do keep in touch with my half-brother Jack and his family. Jack is seven years younger than me, it's hard to believe that Mum was pregnant with him when she left me. What would our lives have been like? We will never know.

She did tell me, that after Brian, her youngest, she got pregnant again, and this time she thought it was a girl because she felt different. Sadly, she miscarried that baby, and she said with each baby she had, she was hoping for a girl. To replace me. Why? I was still her daughter. So you see, with so many questions, and so many blank spaces in her mind where the answers should be, it was very hard to bond.

She once asked me "Do you forgive me," I said I did. But did I?

Epilogue

How did I feel about writing this book? Upset of course, but I knew I had to do it. Mum always said "you should write a book, you write such lovely letters." I would always write about four or five pages of news, and she said she always loved reading them.

We did have fourteen years together, and I did love her. Whether or not you can say we bonded that well, I don't know. We did have some good and happy times together, but she died with too many questions unanswered. I did ask her things, but most of her answers were a chuckled "Oh, I don't know," she had simply blanked out all the answers.

I wanted to know the answers to questions like; why did she leave? She surely knew she would always have the support of her family? Why didn't she write or keep in touch with Auntie Mary - or Nell, as she called her - Mary was the only sister who was still living in the same place after Mum had left. Why keep it from her own family? I'm sure they would have understood as adults and maybe they would have helped her to find me.

I have closure now. I can enjoy the rest of my life with my husband and our wonderful families.

Greg and I, January 2015

Acknowledgements

The most important person I have to thank is my lovely husband, Greg, who has given me his help and support throughout the years of writing this book.

A very big thank you must go to my cousins, Pam Tappenden and Rita Miles who both supplied me with so many photographs and stories. We had such fun in the afternoons with tea and cake and tears and laughter too.

Thanks to Gerald Hornsby for the invaluable advice on self-publishing, layout and formatting.

And last of all, my thanks must go to Mum, who told me in no uncertain terms, "Write that book!"

Printed in Great Britain
by Amazon